W9-BNV-873

A CHILD'S INTRODUCTION TO The Environment

A CHILD'S INTRODUCTION TO The Environment

The Air, Earth, and Sea Around Us—
Plus Experiments, Projects, and Activities
YOU Can Do to Help Our Planet!

By Michael Driscoll & Professor Dennis Driscoll
Illustrated by Meredith Hamilton

BLACK DOG
& LEVENTHAL
PUBLISHERS
NEW YORK

ISBN-13: 978-1-57912-429-8

Library of Congress Cataloging-in-Publication Data

Driscoll, Michael, 1973-
A child's introduction to the environment: the air, earth, and sea around us: plus experiments, projects, and activities you can do to help our planet!/by Michael Driscoll & Dennis Driscoll; illustrated by Meredith Hamilton.
p. cm.
Includes bibliographical references and index.
ISBN 978-1-57912-429-8 (alk. paper)
1. Environmental sciences—Experiments—Juvenile literature. 2. Environmentalism—Juvenile literature.
I. Driscoll, Dennis M. II. Hamilton, Meredith, ill. III. Title.

GE115.D75 2008
333.72—dc22
2007043422

Cover and interiors: Sheila Hart Design

Manufactured in China

Published by
Black Dog & Leventhal Publishers, Inc.
151 West 19th Street
New York, New York 10011

Distributed by
Workman Publishing Company
225 Varick Street
New York, NY 10014

d f g e c

Disclaimer

All experiments and projects in this book should be undertaken only with adult supervision. Neither the authors nor the publisher accept any responsibility for damage to either persons or possessions which might result from their use.

Acknowledgments

The authors wish to thank Meredith Hamilton for her delightful illustrations, Sheila Hart for her wonderful design, Laura Ross for her enthusiasm and editorial oversight, and J.P. Leventhal for the opportunity.
Special thanks to Rita Barol, the Natural Resources Defense Council, and the Healthy Schools Network for permission to include the poster.

For Aaron,
and for Lucy's younger brother
or sister
–M.D., D.D.

For Austin, Margot, and Celia
–M.H.

Contents

Our Wonderful World

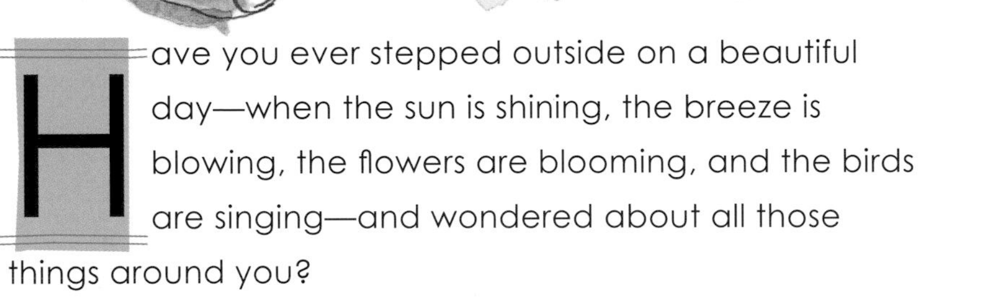

Have you ever stepped outside on a beautiful day—when the sun is shining, the breeze is blowing, the flowers are blooming, and the birds are singing—and wondered about all those things around you?

Maybe you've heard that the flower and the bird rely on each other, but you don't know why. The truth is, everything on the Earth—flowers, birds, and wind included—is connected in important ways.

I'm Professor Driscoll, and I'll be your guide as we explore the *environment*, which is the word we use to describe all the things around us and how they interact.

We'll learn about the Earth's oceans and the animals that live there. We'll explore cities, farms, deserts, and rain forests on land. We'll study the air around us and the interesting things (such as tornadoes!) it sometimes brings. And that's just the beginning.

We'll learn about how the environment helps us and about how we can help protect the environment—first by understanding the changes that are taking place around us, and then by exploring some things we can do to make our planet a better place.

If all of this learning sounds a little bit boring—don't worry! One of the best ways to learn is to try things yourself, and there are lots of fun things to try in this book. Michael—my son, and a budding scientist himself—has come up with a bunch of "Discover for Yourself!" experiments to try at home or at school. He'll also show you ways you can be an environmentalist—someone who helps take care of the environment—in the "How You Can Help" and "Save the Earth!" sections.

Did you look inside the envelope at the front of the book? We've included a poster from a group of kids called the Green Squad (part of a grownup group called the Natural Resources Defense Council), a reusable sack for carrying your lunch to school, and stickers to remind you, your friends, and your family about ways to save energy and help the Earth.

One more thing: Throughout the book, we've put any new or tricky words in **bold** type as a signal that you can look up what they mean in the "Words for the Wise" section at the back.

Enough talk—let's get going. We have a whole world to explore!

Talking on Water

"Water, water, everywhere..." a famous poet once said, and he was right. Water may not *seem* to be everywhere, but it is, even when we can't see or feel it. Water exists in three forms: as a liquid (what we usually think of as "water"); as a gas (water vapor); and as a solid (ice).

Water can be found as a liquid in oceans, lakes, and rivers. It also falls as a liquid —in raindrops—and exists as much tinier drops in clouds. What we see when we look at a cloud is really billions of very small water droplets.

Water exists as water vapor in the atmosphere—the air that surrounds the Earth. It's an invisible gas. In fact, all of the gases that make up the atmosphere are invisible—otherwise we couldn't see through it!

Ice can be found in very cold places such as the polar ice caps—or in the snowflakes and icicles you see in wintertime, if you live in a place that gets cold enough.

Evaporation and Condensation

Water can change from one form to another— from solid, to liquid, to gas, and back again. You probably already know what it's called when water changes from a liquid to a solid: that's freezing, like when you put water into an ice tray to make ice.

When water changes from a liquid to a gas, the process is called **evaporation**. When it changes from a gas to a liquid, it is called **condensation**.

When you boil a pot of water on the stove, it heats up and turns into water vapor. That's evaporation.

The same thing happens when you see a puddle disappear slowly on a warm afternoon. As the water heats, it turns to gas. Little by little, the puddle vanishes.

Condensation is just the opposite. Think about holding a glass with an icy-cold drink in it. Ever notice how water forms on the outside? The cold surface of the glass cools the air around it. That turns the surrounding water vapor from a gas into small drops on the side of the glass.

In the same way, air, and the water vapor in it, cools as it is lifted from the surface of the Earth. If the vapor is cooled enough as it rises, it turns into drops of water and forms the clouds you see in the sky.

SAVE THE EARTH!

LEAKY FAUCETS CAN WASTE UP TO 20 GALLONS (76 LITERS) OF WATER A DAY! IF YOU SEE A DRIP, ASK YOUR PARENTS IF YOU CAN HELP FIX IT.

The Salty Seas

About 70 percent of the planet Earth is covered by water—mostly liquid but some ice, too—and almost all of that water can be found in the Earth's major oceans: the Atlantic, the Pacific, the Arctic, and the Indian oceans.

All of the planet's waters—whether in lakes, oceans, or rivers—have some salt in them, but the oceans have a lot. Why? When ocean water evaporates and turns into water vapor, it leaves the salt behind. This water vapor will later condense into cloud droplets, which then turn into raindrops (or snow, where it is cold) and fall to the ground as **freshwater**.

Small amounts of salt in the ground are absorbed by the water that flows from the ground into lakes, rivers, and ponds. Then, the freshwater finds its way back to the ocean through rivers and streams—and it brings that little bit of salt it absorbed from the ground with it. So the ocean slowly gets saltier and saltier, just as your piggy bank slowly fills up as you put in a little money from time to time. (As long as you don't take any out!)

HOLD THE SALT!

REMOVING SALT FROM SEAWATER ISN'T JUST FOR SAILORS. SOME CITIES, SUCH AS TAMPA, FLORIDA, USE THE PROCESS TO HELP PROVIDE THE WATER THAT FLOWS INTO HOMES.

Discover for Yourself
Removing Salt from Saltwater

Have you ever wondered how to get the salt out of saltwater so it's safe for drinking? The oceans are filled with saltwater–but it can make you sick if you drink it, so scientists have figured out a way to turn the salty seawater into something drinkable. You can do the same thing at home.

You'll need:
- 2 cups (500 ml) tap water
- ½ teaspoon (2 ½ gr) salt
- A large bowl
- A glass not quite as tall as the bowl
- Plastic wrap
- Tape
- A penny

1. Add the salt to the water from your kitchen faucet. Stir it so the salt dissolves.
2. Place the glass in the middle of the bowl. Make sure the top of the glass doesn't quite reach the top of the bowl.
3. Pour the tap water into the bowl, making sure not to pour any into the glass.
4. Cover the bowl with plastic wrap. Use tape to make sure it's sealed all the way around.
5. Put the penny in the center of the plastic wrap, just over the drinking glass.
6. Put the bowl in a spot where it will get direct sunlight for a week and be careful not to move it.
7. Remove the plastic wrap and take a sip of the water in the glass. No salt!

What happened? Evaporation, that's what! When the sun heated it, the water began to turn to gas, leaving the salt behind. The gas rose until it bumped into the plastic wrap, which made it turn back into water drops. The droplets slid to the middle (thanks to the penny) and then dripped into the glass, where the water collected, salt free!

SUN

Can You "Sea" the Difference?

We tend to think of oceans as being the same all over the world, but this is not so. The **salinity** (how salty the water is) may be different from one ocean to another. Temperature is another difference—waters are warmer in some places than in others. Some ocean waters are much deeper than others, and there are differences in the plants and animals that live in the oceans. The movement of surface waters known as **currents** differ, too.

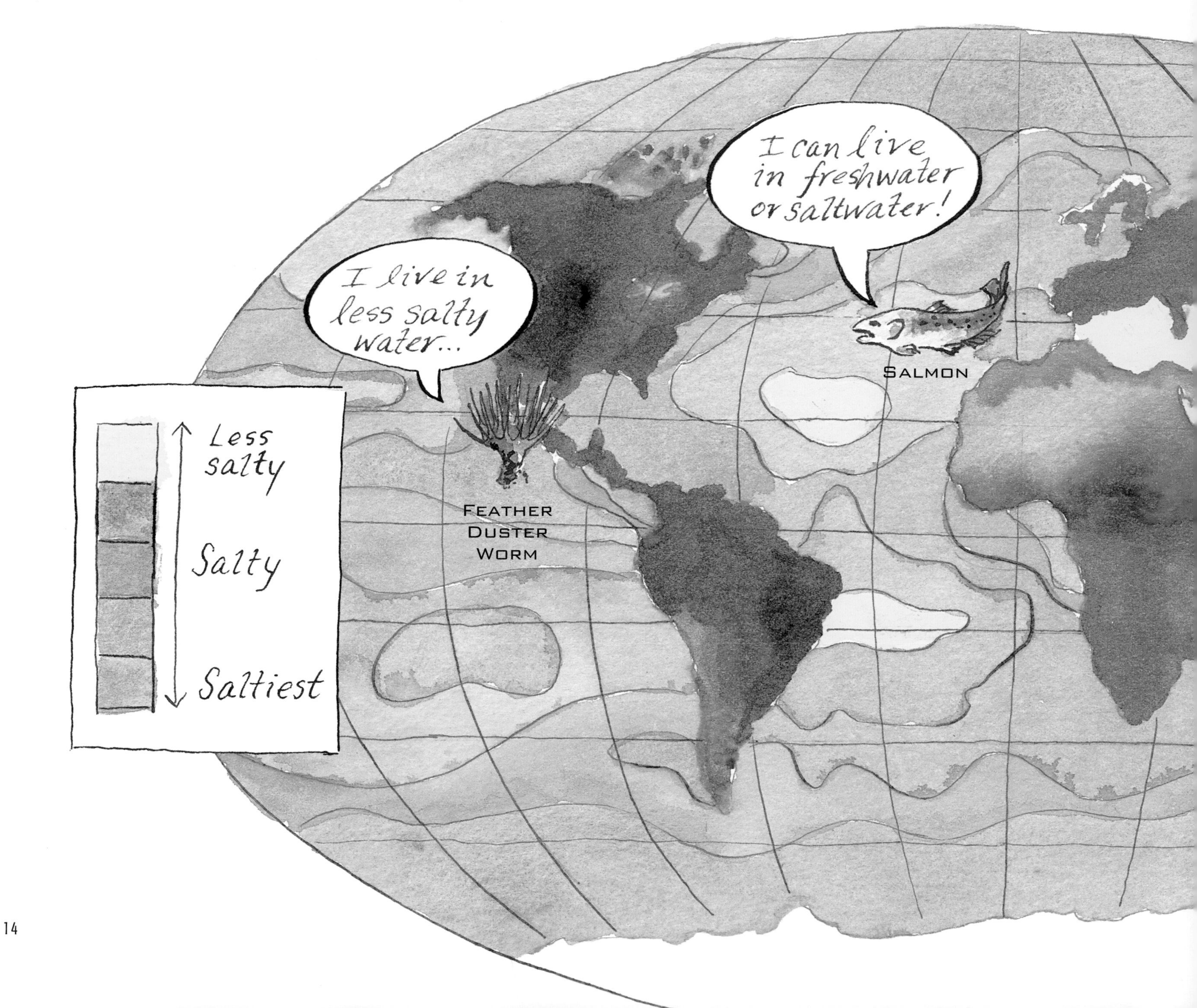

The ocean usually gets deeper as you move away from the shoreline. We measure the depth of the ocean as it compares to what we call **sea level**—the point where the oceans' waters reach the shore. (The height of mountains is measured against sea level, too.)

The deepest place anywhere on Earth is in the western Pacific Ocean, near Japan. It is called the Marianas Trench, and it is 6.8 miles (10.9 kilometers) deep! How deep is that? Well, you would have to stack 29 Empire State Buildings, one on top of the other, to reach from the bottom of the trench to the water's surface. By comparison, the highest mountain on Earth, Mount Everest, is just 5.5 miles (8.8 kilometers) high.

NATURE'S HEATER

HOT SPRINGS ON THE OCEAN FLOOR HELP THE ANIMALS THERE SURVIVE. MINERALS THAT WORMS FEED ON COME OUT OF THESE "VENTS"—AND OTHER ANIMALS FEED ON THE WORMS.

Latitude, which is measured in degrees, is used to tell how far someplace is from the equator. Waters in higher latitudes (nearer the North and South poles) are usually colder than waters in lower latitudes (nearer the equator).

Temperature also changes with depth. The warmest waters are closest to the surface, the area called the Sunlit Zone. Just below, in an area known as the Twilight Zone, only a small amount of sunlight reaches and the waters are colder. Near the bottom of the ocean, an area called the Midnight Zone, there is no light at all, and the waters are really cold—almost freezing!

How YOU can help!

Be a Water-Saver!

While ocean levels are rising, many sources of freshwater are drying up. We can all pitch in and try to use less water–starting with when we brush our teeth. If you normally leave the water running while you polish those pearly whites, you may be sending as much as 8 gallons (32 liters) of water down the drain. By running the water just long enough to wet your toothbrush and then to rinse out afterward, you can cut that to just a ½ gallon (2 liters)!

Here are some other ways to save water:

- Try taking shorter showers.
- Ask your dad not to run the water when he's shaving–just up fill the sink and use that water, then empty it when finished.
- Ask your parents to put a brick in the toilet tank. This will reduce the water that is used every time you flush.
- Check all of the faucets in your house–do any of them drip-drip-drip? Let your parents know, so they can tighten them up.
- Do your parents water your lawn and flowers every day? Ask them to cut down to just a few times a week and let the rain do the rest. (Some neighborhoods have developed special watering schedules, where people whose names start with A to M water one day; N to Z, the next. Good idea!)

Can you think of other ways to be a water-saver?

Our Changing Earth: Rising Sea Levels

You've probably heard something about global warming (and you'll read more about it later). It is causing the ice in the higher latitudes and on mountains to melt. This means more water flows into the oceans, causing water levels to rise—just as when you fill the bathtub too high.

Think about it this way: At one time, if you went to the seashore, you had to walk 100 steps from the parking lot to the water's edge. If the sea level rises, you may someday only have to walk 50 steps to reach the water's edge. No big deal, you say? Well, many cities are located near shorelines, so rising ocean levels could mean that parts of cities such as New York, Los Angeles and Sydney could someday be under water. Lots of people are concerned about what will happen if global warming is allowed to continue, and are coming up with ways to slow it down or stop it. (Some ideas for things we can all do to help can be found later in this book!)

POST-GLOBAL WARMING BEACH HOUSE

Water World

Over 2 million **species** of plants and animals can be found on our planet. (A group of plants or animals that share certain similarities are said to be in the same species.) The waters of the world, both fresh and salty, are teeming with an incredible variety of life—from cattail plants growing along the edges of lakes to the giant whales swimming in the great oceans. There are even forms of life we haven't discovered yet!

Lakes, rivers, and other freshwaters are homes to thousands of plant and animal species—40 percent of all species of fish are found in freshwaters.

The CATTAIL is a tall, slender plant with a furry spike at the end. It grows around lakes and other wet places.

Frogs are amphibians. Most **amphibians** begin their life in water, then move onto dry land as they grow older. The BARKING TREE FROG spends its time in trees when it's warm out and burrows into the ground or among plants when it's cold out. Pretty smart!

CATFISH have long barbs growing near their mouths that look like a cat's whiskers. **Fish** are cold blooded and breathe through gills. Catfish are not particularly picky eaters—most will eat just about anything they find—plant or animal.

When an animal is warm blooded, it means it can save or get rid of body heat when it needs to—such as when we sweat to cool ourselves. Cold-blooded animals take on the temperature of their environments, and must move to a different place if it gets too hot or cold—as when snakes warm themselves in the sun or crawl under rocks to cool off.

Can you tell which of the animals below are warm blooded and which are cold blooded? (The answers are at the bottom of the page)

Lizard   Cocker spaniel   Elephant   Cobra   Chimpanzee   Snapping turtle

ALLIGATORS have anywhere from sixty to eighty teeth and can grow to be 20 feet (6 meters) long! Alligators are **reptiles**, cold-blooded animals with scales or hard plates covering their skin. They breathe with lungs just as we do.

HERONS live along the edges of lakes and rivers. As **birds**, they have feathers and beaks and they lay eggs. Herons' long legs allow them to wade through shallow waters so they can spear fish with their sharp beaks.

MANATEES are found in rivers and bays in the Atlantic Ocean. Though they swim with the help of flippers shaped like paddles, they are actually more closely related to elephants than to dolphins or whales. Manatees are **mammals**—they have warm blood and feed milk to their young, just like dogs, cats, and humans.

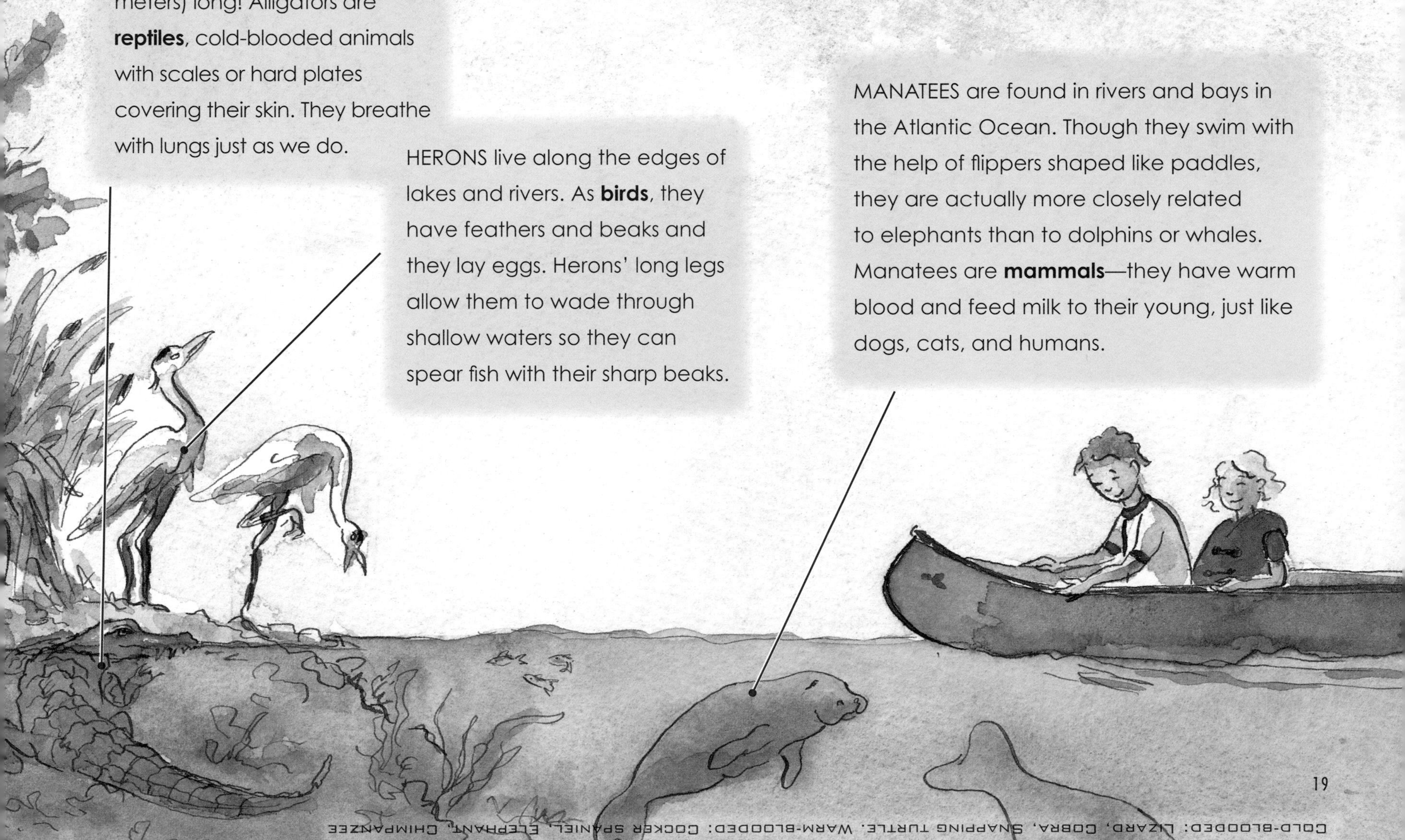

Cold-blooded: Lizard, Cobra, Snapping turtle. Warm-blooded: Cocker spaniel, Elephant, Chimpanzee

The Earth's oceans are home to a great variety of life—from the starfish we collect near the seashore to mysterious creatures with no eyes that lurk near the cold, dark ocean floor. Some are strange looking or downright ugly! Some are beautiful—and all are important to the delicate balance of life on the planet. And whether you're snorkeling at a coral reef or viewing photos on a Web site, everyone can marvel at the wonders of the seas' plants and animals. They are a vital resource worth protecting.

Ah... all alone on the ocean...

Shore Things

The OCTOPUS is a **mollusk**, an animal with a soft body and no spine. It has large eyes and eight tentacles—that's where the "octo-" comes from: it means "eight." Unlike most mollusks, such as clams, the octopus doesn't live in a shell.

MANTA RAYS are fish that live in warm waters and swim by flapping fins that look sort of like wings. One type of manta ray, the giant devil ray, can grow up to 23 feet (8 meters) wide. But don't let the name scare you—devil rays don't usually harm us humans.

SPONGES may look like plants but they're actually very simple animals. They pump water through their bodies and snag the food from it to survive. Some sea sponges can be used for cleaning, but the sponges you find around your house probably weren't made from real sea sponges.

Oceans are home to lots and lots of SEAWEED, which grows from the ocean floor just as flowers and weeds grow on land. There are lots of different kinds of seaweed and seaweed provides food for many creatures—even humans!

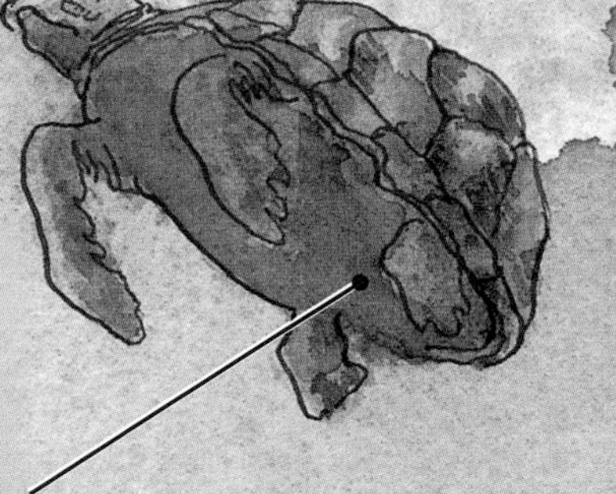

The Open Ocean

Little does SHE know!

SEA TURTLES are reptiles related to the turtles you may have seen in your own backyard or on hikes in the woods. But this turtle is much bigger—some are more than 9 feet (3 meters) long! Their legs are like great paddles and they can use them to swim 300 miles (483 kilometers) in only ten days!

The BLUE WHALE may look like a huge fish but it is a mammal—the largest one ever on the planet—bigger even than the largest dinosaur! It can grow to more than 100 feet (30 meters) long and weigh more than 100 tons. The blue whale has a big appetite but it eats small, feeding on **plankton**, tiny plants and animals that float in the water.

The GREAT WHITE SHARK can grow to be more than 20 feet (6 meters) long. Its massive mouth has rows of sharp teeth that it uses to tear apart its prey, including seals and sea lions.

The scary-looking ANGLERFISH lives in the dark ocean depths, so it makes its own light with an unusual fin that hangs in front of its mouth—and glows! This helps attract other fish that the anglerfish quickly gobbles up.

Our Changing Earth: Endangered Species

As we've learned, there are millions of species of plants and animals on the Earth—but the Earth is constantly changing. There are natural changes, such as the warming and cooling of the planet, that happen over millions of years. And there are man-made changes, such as the creation of cities on land where plants and animals once lived, and the use of automobiles, which can change the air around us.

These changes sometimes cause certain species to die out altogether—they become **extinct**. Natural changes led to the extinction of the dinosaurs many years ago. But many plants and animals have become extinct, or are threatened with extinction in the future, because of things that we humans have done or are doing.

But it's not all bad news. In recent years, many people have worked to save animals before they become extinct—the bald eagle, for example.

There were once nearly 50 million American BISON, also called buffalo, in North America, but American settlers hunted them nearly to extinction, killing all but about one thousand. American bison are no longer found in the wild, but some live in herds kept safe by ranchers and scientists.

Because of hunting and the loss of its ***habitat*** *(the land where it lived), among other problems, by the 1960s there were only 417 known nesting pairs of BALD EAGLES in the forty-eight states of the continental U.S. (all the states except Alaska and Hawaii). But* **conservationists**—*people who help conserve, or save, plants, animals and other natural resources—worked to protect the eagles. By 2007, the number of nesting pairs had grown to nearly ten thousand!*

SAVE THE EARTH!

SCIENTISTS SAY THAT ABOUT 50 SPECIES OF PLANTS AND ANIMALS BECOME EXTINCT EVERY DAY—AND THERE ARE PROBABLY SOME ENDANGERED SPECIES NOT FAR FROM WHERE YOU LIVE. THE FIRST STEP TOWARD HELPING PROTECT THEM IS LEARNING ABOUT THEM. CHECK WITH YOUR LOCAL PARKS OR WILDLIFE AGENCY FOR INFORMATION ON ENDANGERED PLANTS AND ANIMALS NEAR YOUR HOME, AND WHAT YOU CAN DO TO HELP PROTECT THEM.

The GOLDEN TOAD used to live in the nation of Costa Rica, but the last time anyone saw one was in 1989. Scientists don't all agree on what caused the toad to disappear. Some think it lost its habitat as cities grew. Others blame the slow warming of the planet. And some think other animals may have wiped it out.

Because of too much hunting, the BLUE WHALE is considered an endangered species, which means it is in danger of disappearing altogether. Since rules have been put into place to protect the whales, their numbers have increased. We can make a difference!

The ROSY PERIWINKLE is found in the country of Madagascar, but it is disappearing because people there are cutting down the forests it lives in. The rosy periwinkle can be used to treat cancer, so you can see why it's important we protect it—and other species.

Most of us don't think much about it when we turn on the faucet. But where does that water come from? And where does it go once it swirls down the drain?

As we learned earlier, the only water that is safe for drinking is freshwater. So all the water that flows through our pipes at home must come from freshwater sources, either surface water or groundwater. **Surface water** is any water on the surface of the Earth and open to the air, such as the water in lakes and rivers. **Groundwater** is found underground in places where it has collected, called **aquifers**.

Pipes and pumps direct surface water and ground water to filtration plants that remove dirt and other tiny particles. Helpful chemicals may also be added to clean the water further. Once the cleaning process is done, the water is ready to drink. It is sometimes stored in big water towers until we need it.

So what happens once you've finished brushing your teeth and washed the water down the drain? That water goes through your pipes, into the neighborhood sewer system, then right to a sewage treatment plant. There it is cleaned again, using everything from screens that catch big stuff to chemicals and bacteria that remove smaller stuff. Once the water has been cleaned, it's sent back out into our lakes, rivers, and other freshwater sources—so it can someday make the trip back to your faucet again!

THE CHEMICAL KNOWN AS FLUORIDE IS OFTEN ADDED TO WATER SYSTEMS TO HELP PREVENT TOOTH DECAY. IT'S A LITTLE LIKE BRUSHING YOUR TEETH EVERY TIME YOU TAKE A DRINK! (BUT ONLY A LITTLE—YOU SHOULD STILL BRUSH OFTEN.)

DISCOVER for YOURSELF
Test the Water

Here's a fun and easy way to figure out whether you're using more water than necessary in the shower.

All you'll need is:

- An empty 1 quart (1 liter) milk container
- And a watch.

1. Open the top of the milk container so that you can fill it easily with water.

2. Stand in the shower and turn the water on to a normal flow. (You may want to wear a bathing suit so you don't get your clothes wet–or do this at your regular shower time.)

3. Hold the container underneath the shower head for 10 seconds. If you have a waterproof watch you can count them out yourself, or you can get someone to stand outside the shower and count for you. If your carton overflows in under 10 seconds, your shower head is spraying too much water and you are wasting a vital natural resource. A special "low-flow" shower head can help. These mix air with the water so you get nearly the same pressure but use much less water. Or you can just turn down those faucets.

Going with the Flow

Energy Essentials

It's hard to imagine but, just a few hundred years ago, power as we know it didn't exist. There were no streetlamps. No automobiles. No air conditioners and no furnaces. No electric guitars! Most people got up at daybreak and went to bed not long after sunset because, once it was dark out, it was hard to see. Everything had to be done by the light of candles or oil lamps.

But that all changed as scientists began to make advances in the study of **electricity**—a form of energy produced by tiny charged particles. The common lightbulb was invented in 1879 by Thomas Edison, and a few years later he opened the first central power station. Then power could be produced and a network of power lines could deliver it to homes and businesses to light up those lightbulbs.

Once electricity became available, people couldn't get enough of it. More and more uses were developed for electricity and, as the Earth's population grew, more and more people demanded power. That power has to come from somewhere, and producing enough of it to meet everyone's demands has become one of the great challenges of our time.

AFTER-DINNER SING, 1840

AFTER-DINNER SING, NOW

SAVE THE EARTH!

DID YOU KNOW THAT IF A SINGLE GALLON (4 LITERS) OF SPILLED PAINT SEEPS INTO THE GROUND, IT CAN CONTAMINATE 250,000 GALLONS (1 MILLION LITERS) OF DRINKING WATER? THAT'S WHY IT'S SO IMPORTANT NOT TO SPILL CHEMICALS INTO THE GROUND, WHERE THEY CAN SEEP INTO THE GROUNDWATER. WHEN IT COMES TIME TO THROW AWAY PAINT OR OTHER LIQUIDS THAT COULD HARM THE ENVIRONMENT, ALWAYS FOLLOW THE DISPOSAL INSTRUCTIONS ON THE CONTAINER—OR BETTER YET, ASK AN ADULT FOR HELP.

Power to the People

One kind of power (we'll learn about others later) is hydroelectric power, which uses the flow of water to generate energy. Dams such as the Hoover Dam, on the border between Arizona and Nevada, have been built to control the flow of water in rivers. As water is allowed to run through the dam, the force of its flow turns special machines called **generators** that produce power.

Water Works

One of the great things about hydroelectric power is that it produces no **pollution**—it doesn't create waste that dirties the land, air or water. It's also **renewable**, which means it doesn't get used up like some other power sources we'll learn about. But there's a catch: Hydroelectric generators can only be built in places where there's lots of flowing water, usually mountainous areas with fast-flowing rivers. And those dams cause lots of water to build up behind them, flooding places that wild plants and animals (not to mention people!) once called home. They also keep some fish from returning to waters where they once laid their eggs.

NO-POWER HOUR

WANT TO SEE JUST HOW MUCH WE RELY ON POWER SOURCES? TRY TO GO WITHOUT IT FOR A LITTLE WHILE BY ORGANIZING AN HOUR WITHOUT POWER AT YOUR HOUSE. GET YOUR WHOLE FAMILY TO SPEND ONE HOUR DOING THINGS THAT REQUIRE NO ELECTRICITY OR GASOLINE POWER. YOU'LL GET A TASTE OF WHAT LIFE WAS LIKE JUST A HUNDRED OR SO YEARS AGO. OF COURSE THIS MEANS DOING WITHOUT TELEVISION AND VIDEO GAMES. YOU MIGHT TRY READING INSTEAD, BUT BETTER DO IT DURING THE DAYLIGHT NEAR A WINDOW—NO LAMPS TO LIGHT THOSE PAGES. PLAYING IN THE PARK MIGHT SOUND LIKE A GOOD IDEA, BUT YOU'LL HAVE TO RIDE YOUR BIKE TO GET THERE. FORGET ABOUT A SNACK, TOO, UNLESS IT'S SOMETHING OUT OF THE CUPBOARD. NO DRINKS FROM THE REFRIGERATOR OR COOKIES FROM THE OVEN. YOUR HOUR WITHOUT POWER MAY SEEM LONGER THAN YOU THOUGHT—BUT IT'S A GREAT WAY TO REMIND OURSELVES JUST HOW MUCH WE RELY ON POWER IN OUR WORLD, AND HOW MUCH OF IT WE USE.

So, then the ghost TOOK the bone and...

The Land We Live On

About one-third of the Earth is covered by land. The very large land masses are called continents—there are seven of them. The smaller bits of land are called islands (although you could say that the continents themselves are really very large islands). Land is made of solid material, but the uppermost part—the part we walk on—is mostly soil, a mixture of rock and organic (or living) material.

In addition to lakes, streams, and other wet areas that dot the land surface, there is vegetation, or plants. Some of this living material has grown up naturally (forests, for example) and some has been planted by us humans (vegetable and flower gardens, for instance). Of course, people have made other additions to the planet's surface. Cities, towns, and the roads that run between them take up more and more space every day.

The surface of the Earth is very different from place to place. There are hills, mountains, and flat, wide-open plains. There are jungles and forests. There are dry deserts and there are marshes, which are wet areas where rivers meet larger bodies of water. And one continent, Antarctica, is covered almost entirely by ice!

OUT WITH THE OLD

The changes taking place on the Earth aren't just things that happen elsewhere. If you've lived in your city or town long enough, you've probably seen changes there: a new office building where a park used to be; a parking lot on land that was empty; a new shopping mall alongside a new highway. If you want to go further back, talk to an older person who's lived in the area for a long time. Ask him what he remembers from years ago, and how your community has changed over many years. Then consider how those changes affect the environment. Remember that changes—good and bad—are happening everywhere, all the time.

SAVE THE EARTH!

Don't throw away those old toys or clothes. Donate them so they can be used by others. That's a form of recycling—and you will be helping someone less fortunate than you.

Two hundred years ago, about one out of every twenty people in the world lived in a city. Now about half of the world's population does. Cities have become important places for creating products that are sent elsewhere, but they also rely on bringing in items made or grown in other places. That's one reason that many of our largest cities are on the shores of oceans or rivers: the water provides an easy way to move all of that stuff in and out.

In cities, people live close together, which can create special problems. Planners must find ways to bring food, water, and power to all these people, and to get rid of their waste products. But cities have their own special benefits, too. There are lots of jobs in cities, as well as stores to shop in, museums to visit, and fun things such as concerts and ball games to go to. (Smaller communities have these things, too, but not as many.)

Just outside of most cities are communities known as **suburbs** (short for suburban areas, because they are smaller than cities or urban areas). They are not quite as tightly packed as cities, offering more space for bigger homes and yards. Because suburbs are near big cities, the people who live in suburbs can travel easily to those cities to work, shop, or just have fun.

Living in the City

SQUIRRELS have bushy tails and can be found living in trees. They eat nuts, seeds, and fruit, and sometimes bury these treasures in the ground during the fall, saving them for the winter months, when food can be hard to find.

FLIES can live just about anywhere. Some have a form of taste buds on their feet that tell them whether or not what they've landed on is good to eat!

PEREGRINE FALCONS sometimes make nests high in skyscrapers and feed on squirrels, rats, and pigeons. They can dive at up to 175 miles (280 kilometers) per hour!

The ELM is a hardy tree that thrives in cities. Its upper branches tend to spread out, which makes it great for providing shade.

RATS can live in sewers and will eat almost anything. They have spread from Asia to just about every corner of the world—wherever humans have gone.

BLUEFISH often live in rivers near coastal cities. They get their name from their bluish-gray coloring.

DISCOVER for YOURSELF
Make a Birdfeeder

Want to bring even more birds into your backyard? It's easy to make your own bird feeder that will have them visiting in no time.

You'll need:
- A clean, empty, cardboard milk carton
- Scissors
- Strong twine or wire
- Birdseed
- A big paper clip
- A thin stick

1. Cut two windows, about the size of a standard postcard, on opposite sides of the milk carton.
2. Poke a hole underneath each window.
3. Run a stick through the two holes. This will be the birds' perch.
4. Poke a hole in the top of the milk carton and run the paper clip through it.
5. Tie the string to the paper clip, then hang it from a sturdy tree limb. (You may need a grown-up to help with this part.)
6. Fill the bottom of the carton with birdseed and wait for your new friends to arrive!

DISCOVER for YOURSELF
Be a Bird Watcher

Birds can be found just about everywhere, from wild turkeys in the woods to sea gulls on the beach, to pigeons in the cities. What kinds of birds live in your neighborhood? Take a look outside and find out.

You'll need:
- Binoculars
- A small notebook
- A pen or pencil
- Reference material–a book or Web site with descriptions of the birds common to your area

Bird-watching is simple: Find a good, quiet spot outside, stay very still, and take a look around. Use your ears, too, and listen for different bird calls, chirps, and whistles. Soon, you'll start to recognize a bird by its call as well as how it looks. Use your binoculars to peek into tree branches. If you or a neighbor has a bird feeder, watch what species stop in for a snack. When you spot a bird, write a description of it in your notebook–its color, its size, any unusual markings it has. Draw a picture of it, too. (You can color it in later.)

You might want to describe the sound of its birdsong, whether it's a high whistle, a deep squawk, or something else altogether. It takes patience.

After you've collected notes on the birds you find, check your references and see if you can identify them. Read about their habits and their habitats. You've just learned more about the world around you! Some people keep track of the birds they see all their lives, wherever they go, and call it a "life list." Now is a great time to start one!

Power to the People: Fossil Fuels

About 85 percent of the energy we use is supplied by fossil fuels—or coal, natural gas, and oil. These energy needs include everything from making a lightbulb glow to fueling the family car to powering your favorite roller coaster at the amusement park.

Fossils are the remains of things that were once living, and fossil fuels come from dead plants and animals, called organic material. When a living thing dies—whether it's a mouse or a bug or a tree—its remains return to the ground as organic material. As time goes by, the organic material piles up and is pressed deeper and deeper toward the Earth's warmer core. Over millions and millions of years, that great heat and great pressure turn the organic material into coal, gas, or oil.

SAVE THE EARTH!

Hot water sure is nice when it comes time to take a shower. But guess how that water got warm? That's right—it took power to warm it up in your home's hot-water heater. So be careful when you use that hot water. Don't leave the shower running without you as it heats up. Once it's warm enough, climb in! If you're taking a bath, don't fill the tub to the top. You can get just as clean with the tub one-third of the way filled. Remember, the less hot water you use, the less power you're using—and that's better for the Earth.

Coal is simply a kind of rock—like sandstone, granite, or marble—that can be dug out of the ground. If it's far under the surface, we have to tunnel to get to it.

Oil doesn't exist in underwater pools, as you might think. It is contained within rocks.

Imagine how a sponge soaks up water. Certain rocks contain oil in the same way.

Natural gas (not to be confused with gasoline, which is a processed fuel) is also found in certain kinds of rocks. Gas and oil are harder to get to than coal, and sometimes require very deep drilling into the Earth—even into the bottom of the oceans!

The Story of FOSSIL FUELS...

LIVING things—plants and animals—die, and their remains return to Earth ...

Once we've gotten the coal, oil, or gas out of the ground, there are a number of ways we use it. Coal can be burned to make heat. That heat can turn water into steam, and the steam can turn generators that provide electricity. Gas can be burned to heat air so that the air can turn generators. And oil can by turned into the gasoline we use to fuel our cars.

BENEATH the Earth's surface, those remains pile up...

OVER millions of years, heat and pressure turn them into gas, coal—or oil!

As we've learned, cities are home to lots of people—millions and millions sometimes—and they all have to move around. That can be tricky.

In some places, people mostly use cars to travel to work, to the store, to visit a friend, or to make other trips. But in cities, where so many people live so close together, there's just not enough room for everyone to drive—the streets would be packed. So city planners have developed unique ways to move people around. This is called **mass transit**, or transportation methods for moving large numbers (masses) of people.

SAVE THE EARTH!

In some cities, planners have tried to encourage people to leave their cars at home and use mass transit instead. This helps get rid of traffic jams and reduces the harmful substances that cars produce. In London, England, drivers have to pay a fee to enter the main parts of the city by car during the busiest times. This has led to an average of 60,000 fewer cars in those areas every day. Officials in New York City are considering the same kind of system.

Trolleys were an early method of moving people around within cities, and are still in use today in some places, such as San Francisco. Trolleys run like trains, over tracks along city streets, and the trolley cars can hold many more people than a family car can. People climb aboard at one stop, then get off when they've reached their destination.

Cities on the Move

Subways are like trolleys except they run underground. Entrances and exits are scattered around cities, and riders climb down steps (or use escalators or elevators) to reach the platforms where the trains arrive and depart.

Because subways run underground (that's where the "sub" comes from: it means "under"), they take up very little space and can move many people around quickly. The subway system in Tokyo, Japan, runs along thirteen different lines and transports more than 7 million people every day.

Cities are busy places with many people, but **rural** communities are just the opposite: they have lots of land, but fewer people live there.

When you think about rural areas, you probably think of farms and ranches. But rural areas also include forests, national parks, mountains, deserts—any place where the environment has been left in its natural state, changed very little by man.

WOODPECKERS use their stiff beaks to make holes in trees, where they build nests and find food. Their thick skulls protect them from the heavy bang-bang-bang of their pecking.

The Rural Life

MAPLE TREES grow in many places throughout North America. Their strong wood is great for building houses—and the sticky goo or sap inside them is used to make the maple syrup we put on pancakes.

RACCOONS are forest creatures that eat berries, seeds, and acorns. They also hunt for frogs and fish in streams and rivers, and have been known to rinse off their food before eating it!

BLACK BEARS eat fish, berries, and honey. They store up food during the autumn months for the long winter naps they take, known as **hibernation**.

LARGE-MOUTH BASS live in rural lakes and rivers. They're not the tastiest fish to eat, but are prized by fishermen for the fierce fight they put up when caught. (Nowadays, lots of fishermen release the fish they catch back into the water, anyway—they like to fish for fun, but they don't want to harm or kill the fish!)

Feeding the World (and the Farmers Who Do)

Early farmers are believed to have collected their first harvests around 8000 BC. Back then, they raised just enough food to feed their families, with perhaps a little left over to sell to others. Later, farmers raised animals as well as plants. Those who raise animals are now known as ranchers.

But much has changed in the ten thousand years since the days of the first farmers. Today, most farmers specialize in specific **crops**—certain kinds of plants, such as rice, lettuce, watermelons, or oranges. And they grow them not for their own use, but to sell to others. Ranchers do the same with cows, sheep, chickens, or pigs.

Farmers and ranchers carefully select where they raise their crops. For farmers, the land must be **fertile**—it must be a good place for the seeds to take root and grow. For ranchers, the land must provide a good home for the animals they'll raise. A cattle rancher, for instance, needs lots of room for his cattle to roam, with lots of grass for them to feed on.

FARMER, 1000 A.D.

HOW DOES *YOUR* GARDEN GROW?

YOU DON'T HAVE TO LIVE IN THE COUNTRY TO START YOUR OWN "FARM"—YOU CAN DO IT YOURSELF BY STARTING A GARDEN. YOU'LL NEED A SMALL AREA OF LAND IN YOUR YARD, OR PERHAPS JUST A WINDOW BOX THAT CAN HOLD A FEW PLANTS. A LOCAL GARDENING CENTER CAN HELP YOU PICK OUT THE SOIL AND SEEDS YOU'LL NEED, AND CAN ALSO PROVIDE INSTRUCTIONS FOR GROWING YOUR "CROPS." PEAS, TOMATOES, AND CARROTS ARE ALL FAIRLY EASY TO GROW—AND GREAT TO EAT, TOO! WINDOW BOXES ARE ESPECIALLY GOOD FOR HERBS SUCH AS BASIL, PARSLEY, AND DILL.

Where Did **YOUR** Breakfast Come From?

Hot Chocolate (Costa Rica)

Egg (Regional chicken farm)

Milk (Regional dairy farm)

Butter (California dairy farm)

Orange Juice (Florida citrus grove)

Bread (Indiana wheat)

Cantaloupe (South Texas)

Blueberries (Maine)

Unless you live on a farm where you grow your own food, nearly everything you eat today can be traced back to a farm or ranch somewhere. If you had eggs for breakfast this morning, they came from a ranch where chickens are raised. If you ate cornflakes, you can bet that a farmer somewhere grew that corn. And the milk you drank came from the cows on a dairy farm.

The Cycle of Life

Every plant or animal on the Earth is linked in one way or another to its environment. Most plants rely on sunlight, carbon dioxide, and water to make their own food through a process called **photosynthesis**. Some of the carbon dioxide plants use comes from humans and other animals—carbon dioxide (along with water vapor) is what we breathe out when we exhale. And just as we exhale carbon dioxide, the process of photosynthesis causes plants to release oxygen, which we breathe in. We couldn't live without plants, and plants couldn't live without us!

Plants also make up the first level of what's known as the "food chain." Animals that eat only plants are called **herbivores**. Some herbivores are small, such as beetles, though others are quite large, such as elephants and panda bears. **Carnivores** are the next step on the food chain—animals that eat other animals to survive. Most of us people (and some other animals as well) eat both plants and meat, which makes us **omnivores**.

The waste that living things—plants, herbivores, and carnivores—release back into the Earth when they die helps nourish new plants . . . which are eaten by herbivores . . . which are eaten by carnivores. And the cycle continues.

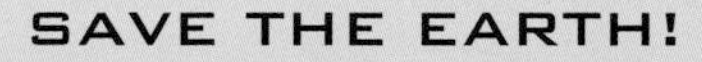

SAVE THE EARTH!

WANT TO GET TO KNOW THE ANIMALS THAT LIVE IN YOUR AREA BETTER? TRY STARTING A BRUSH PILE IN YOUR BACKYARD. (GET YOU PARENTS' PERMISSION, FIRST.) OLD LOGS, LEAVES, BRANCHES FROM TREES AND BUSHES—THESE ARE ALL THINGS ANIMALS LOVE TO HIDE UNDERNEATH. START A BRUSH PILE IN YOUR YARD AND CHECK EVERY NOW AND THEN TO SEE WHO'S COME TO VISIT YOU.

THESE are the plants...

that were eaten by a grasshopper...

that was eaten by a snake...

that was eaten by an owl...

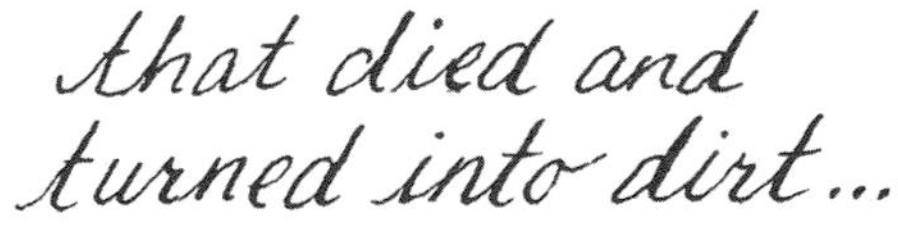

that died and turned into dirt...

SAVE THE EARTH!

Don't fill up the landfill! Take a look around your house and think about things you could reuse rather than throw away. Bags are an easy one, and boxes, too—a giant cardboard box makes a great clubhouse. Most bottles can be cleaned out and used again to hold water or juice. Remember that paper has two sides—when you are drawing, writing or coloring, use both sides of the paper. What items do you think you might be able to save from going to the landfill? Make a list. (You'll save your family money by reusing things, too.)

From Trash Can to Landfill

In the year 2005, Americans threw away more than 245 million tons of waste. That's a huge amount! Divided up among every grown-up and child in the country, that's

about 4½ pounds (2 kilograms) of waste coming from each person, every single day. If you had to carry that weight around, it would be enough to fill up your backpack every other day. That's something to think about the next time you toss an empty juice box into the kitchen trash can.

But where does all that waste go? We know sanitation workers pick it up from our curb every week and toss it into giant trucks, but then what?

Some of our waste gets recycled. (We'll learn about that later.) Some of it gets taken to what we think of as "dumps"—those stinky mountains of trash where waste slowly piles higher and higher. And some of our waste is burned, which can release harmful substances into the atmosphere.

But most of our trash goes to a landfill. **Landfills** are places where trash is buried between layers of dirt. Landfills are designed to keep the oozy parts of the trash from leaking into the ground—if they did, they could harm the environment. But that doesn't mean that landfills are a great way to get rid of our waste. As we learned, we're constantly producing more and more trash, and when a landfill gets filled up, we have to find a new place to put trash. So more and more land has to be used as the final resting place for those milk jugs, worn-out sneakers, and broken televisions we've thrown away.

How **YOU** *can help!*

Trimming Paper Use

One way to protect the Earth's trees is by reducing the amount of mail your family receives. Many businesses, such as phone companies and banks, allow you to pay bills online. This means no bills sent to your house and no checks your parents need to send back. Every bill paid online means less paper used. And you'll save the cost of a stamp, too! If your parents have a computer and they aren't already paying bills online, ask them to look into it. Tell them it's to help the Earth.

Another form of wasted paper that you can cut down on is "junk mail" –advertisements, catalogs, donation requests, and the like. It's estimated that every family receives the equivalent of one and a half trees worth of junk mail every year. Write to the Direct Marketing Association at Mail Preference Service, P.O. Box 282, Carmel, NY 10512, to ask about being taken off mailing lists. You can also find them online at www.dmaconsumers.org. Ask your parents to contact any charities they support, too, with a request that your address not be shared with other charities. This will cut down on the requests for donations your family receives.

And remember, when you do receive mail–advertisements, bills, whatever–recycle it when you are done with it!

Reuse and Recycle!

As we've learned, a lot of the waste we produce ends up dirtying the environment. But there's a better way to handle much of that garbage: recycling. Many of the things we throw away can be used again—they can be recycled into new products.

Recycling is a win-win: First, garbage that can be recycled doesn't get burned or added to a dump or landfill somewhere, hurting the environment. Second, when we recycle materials, it means we don't have to use up fresh resources to produce something.

Many communities have recycling programs that make it possible for certain materials to be reused. Metal products—soup cans, aluminum foil, wire hangers, even cabinets—can be melted down, then used to make new metal products. Glass bottles and jars can be recycled in the same way. Paper and cardboard can be recycled to make new paper products and save new trees from being cut down. Some plastic items—such as milk jugs and juice containers—are often recycled, too.

SAVE THE EARTH!

FIND OUT WHAT RECYCLING PROGRAMS YOUR COMMUNITY USES AND ENCOURAGE YOUR FAMILY TO PARTICIPATE. HELP SEPARATE THE THINGS THAT YOUR LOCAL SANITATION DEPARTMENT RECYCLES FROM THE MATERIALS THAT CAN'T BE RECYCLED, AND FIND THE SCHEDULE FOR WHEN RECYCLED PRODUCTS ARE PICKED UP. IT'S ANOTHER WAY YOU CAN DO YOUR PART TO HELP SAVE THE EARTH!

How YOU can help! A Class Act

The school cafeteria is a great place to think about recycling, and there are lots of ways to do it. Here are a few:

1. Do you bring your lunch to school? Use the handy, reusable lunch bag that comes with this book–or get a lunch box, if you prefer–rather than wasting a bag every day. Lunch boxes come in cool styles and designs. Find one you'll be proud to carry.

2. Fill that lunch bag or box with reusable containers for things such as juice, cookies, or your sandwich, rather than using foil and plastic bags that have to be thrown away.

3. Choose a peanut butter-and-jelly sandwich for lunch. Forests are often cut down to provide land to raise animals (see page 53), so skipping hamburgers and other lunch meats can save trees.

4. Your school should have separate containers for collecting aluminum, cardboard, and other recyclables. Use them! Encourage your friends to do the same. Every can recycled is one less that has to be produced.

5. Organic material–such as eggshells or vegetable leftovers (but not meat)–can go right back into the ground in a process called composting.

for COMPO

Compost is what forms when organic material is allowed to break down naturally. That stuff decays and can then be added to soil to make it healthier. If your school doesn't have a composting program, try starting one. Talk to a teacher or your principal about making a compost pile where students can toss organic leftovers. That half of a sandwich you didn't eat can help provide food for someone else in the future.

6. Included with this book is a special poster from the Healthy Schools Network and the Green Squad of the Natural Resources Defense Council, an organization that helps the environment in lots of ways. The poster describes some important things you and your friends can do to help protect the environment. Ask your teacher or principal if you can post it in your school and spread the word!

7. Also included with this book are two sheets of stickers that you can put up around your house or at school. They'll remind you, and others, of things you can do to save energy and protect the environment, things like turning off lights, unplugging appliances, and recycling. (Tell your parents and teachers not to worry–the stickers peel off as easily as they stick on!)

The Wild Woods

A forest is an area of the Earth's surface that is covered with trees. The trees and animals found in each forest depend on the soil in that area, the average temperatures, and rainfall amounts, and whether the land is mountainous, hilly, or flat.

GIANT REDWOOD TREES can grow to more than 300 feet (91 meters) tall. That's the length of a football field. Some have trunks that are more than 20 feet (6 meters) wide. They are found in California and Oregon and can live for thousands of years.

WOLVES travel in packs when they are hunting their prey, and are the biggest of the wild dogs.

The PORCUPINE has a sharp, spiky coat that protects it from **predators**, animals that might try to eat it. It's one of the few animals that can eat pine needles.

Coniferous (pronounced cone-IF-er-us) forests are found at the highest latitudes, farthest from the equator and closest to the North and South poles. The trees in coniferous forests don't lose their needles in winter, which is why we call them **evergreens**.

Deciduous (pronounced de-SID-you-us) forests are generally found closer to the equator than coniferous forests are. Trees in deciduous forests shed their leaves in the fall and grow new leaves the following spring.

AN **ECOSYSTEM** IS A COLLECTION OF LIVING THINGS AND THE ENVIRONMENT IN WHICH THEY LIVE. OUR PLANET CAN BE SEEN AS ONE BIG ECOSYSTEM, ALL OF ITS PLANTS AND CREATURES RELYING ON ONE ANOTHER FOR SURVIVAL. THERE ARE SMALLER ECOSYSTEMS, TOO. FOR EXAMPLE, PRAIRIE ECOSYSTEM INCLUDES COYOTES, THE RABBITS ON WHICH THEY FEED, AND THE GRASSES THAT FEED THE RABBITS.

DEER are graceful creatures whose speed helps them escape from predators. The males fight with their great, wide antlers to become leaders of their herds.

Many plants need lots of sunlight to survive, but FERNS thrive on the shady floors of deciduous forests.

QUAIL make their nests on the ground—and would rather walk than fly. They eat insects and seeds and travel in flocks.

R**ain forests** are found closest to the equator, where it is rainy a lot of the time. They are always warm and wet, and they have no winter so their plants grow all year long. Rain forests are home to more than half of the world's species of plants and animals—even though they cover only 7 percent of the Earth's land.

DISAPPEARING RAIN FORESTS

RAIN FORESTS HAVE ALWAYS COVERED GREAT STRETCHES OF THE EARTH, BUT THEY ARE SHRINKING FAST. SCIENTISTS ESTIMATE THAT MORE THAN 37 MILLION ACRES (150,000 SQUARE KILOMETERS) OF RAIN FOREST ARE LOST EVERY YEAR. THAT'S AN AREA THE SIZE OF THE STATE OF GEORGIA.

WHAT'S HAPPENING? WE'VE ALREADY LEARNED THAT FARMERS AND RANCHERS NEED FERTILE GROUND TO RAISE THEIR CROPS. THE EARTH IS BIG, BUT THERE'S ONLY SO MUCH LAND AVAILABLE, SO RAIN FORESTS ARE BEING CUT DOWN TO MAKE ROOM FOR MORE FARMS AND RANCHES. MINERS WANT TO HUNT FOR PRECIOUS METALS, SUCH AS SILVER, COPPER, AND GOLD, IN AREAS COVERED BY RAIN FORESTS. AND THERE'S ALWAYS A DEMAND FOR THE TIMBER FROM THE TREES THAT MAKE UP THE RAIN FORESTS. AS THE EARTH'S POPULATION GROWS, MORE BUILDINGS ARE NEEDED FOR ALL THOSE PEOPLE TO LIVE AND WORK IN, AND WOOD IS NEEDED TO BUILD THEM.

THE TALLEST TREES EMERGE, OR RISE ABOVE, IN THE **EMERGENT LAYER**.

Layers of the Rain Forest

THE **CANOPY LAYER** IS WHERE MOST TREETOPS ARE FOUND. THEY PROVIDE SHADE FOR THE LIFE BELOW.

TREE TRUNKS AND CLIMBING PLANTS MAKE UP THE **UNDERSTORY LAYER**.

LEAVES, ROOTS, AND DECAYING ORGANIC MATERIAL CAN BE FOUND ON THE **FOREST FLOOR**.

TAMARINS are strange looking little monkeys. Sadly, some types of tamarins are endangered. They have long hair, sometimes white and sometimes golden orange, and their sharp nails help them hold onto tree branches.

TOUCANS have brightly colored feathers and giant beaks, which they use to eat fruit, bugs, and lizards.

With so many trees so close together, it's a fight for light in the rain forest. PASSION FLOWERS grow on tree branches, where they're able to absorb some of the sun's rays.

GOLIATH BIRD-EATING SPIDERS are the biggest spiders in the world. They eat lizards, snakes, and even small birds.

The ANACONDA is a giant snake—some are more than 15 feet (5 meters) long—that constricts, or squeezes, its prey to death before devouring it. It can go a month between feedings.

DISCOVER *for* YOURSELF
Grow a Tree

Actions by humans can have a big impact on the environment, in good ways and bad. One good—and fun—way you can make an impact is by growing a tree.

We know that trees absorb carbon dioxide and release the oxygen that humans need to survive. By growing your own tree, you can help produce that vital oxygen. Your tree will also help protect the soil from **erosion**, which is what happens when soil and rocks are worn away until the area can no longer support life. Your tree will add something beautiful to the world.

And your tree helps the environment in another big way—a fully grown tree provides shade that can help cut the costs to cool your house in the summer. That can cut the power needed to run an air conditioner by 10 to 50 percent.

What you'll need:

- A tree seedling (a young tree that's not yet 3 feet [1 meter] tall)
- A good place to grow it
- A shovel
- Water

What to do:

1. Find out what types of trees grow in your area. You can find this out from your local public garden or arboretum (a kind of living tree museum), the local parks department, or someone who works as a gardener or at a nursery or gardening center. If you're eager to see results, ask what kind of trees grow quickly and don't need much water.

2. Look into how much space and water your tree will need. Does it only grow in certain types of soil? Does it need to be planted at a certain time of year? Ask what you'll need to do to help your tree grow.

3. Buy your tree seedling from a local greenery or gardening center.

4. Choose a good spot to plant it, a place where it will have plenty of room to grow. Keep in mind that the trunk will grow up, the branches will grow out, and the roots will grow down.

5. Use a small shovel to dig a hole just wide enough to spread the seedling's roots out. It should be just deep enough so that the root collar—where the roots spread out from the stem—is even with the ground.
6. Place your seedling in the hole and spread out its roots.

7. Fill in the hole with the soil you dug out, pressing the dirt firmly back into place. You might want to add some fertilizer or "tree food." (Ask about this before you take your tree home.)

8. Pour a half-gallon of water over the soil to help it settle.

9. Follow any special instructions that your experts may have given you about planting the tree or taking care of it afterward.

10. Watch your seedling grow, and enjoy your contribution to the world's trees!

Going, Going, Gone

For many years, rain forests were cut down for their wood, to dig new mines, or to provide new farmland, without much thought to the harm this does to the Earth. But it does hurt the Earth. As you know, trees absorb carbon dioxide and release oxygen, which has a big effect on the rest of the Earth. Fewer trees mean this balance is lost, which can contribute to global warming. There are also things found in rain forests that can't be found anywhere else, including special plants used to make medicines, and unique creatures such as the tiny pygmy marmoset—a monkey that, when grown, weighs only 3 ounces (93 grams)!

The good news is many people have realized how important rain forests are to us all, and are working to save them. Some land owners are planting new trees as they cut down old ones. You can contribute, too, by helping a group that's working to save the rain forests. And you can try to learn more about the things you and your family buy. If a rain forest had to be cut down so cows could graze—and those cows later became hamburgers—consider eating something that doesn't hurt the environment.

Think these efforts don't add up? In 2007, the Brazilian government announced that the amount of rain forest lost during the previous year was the lowest since they started keeping track in 1988!

Lands of Sand

Deserts are the driest places on Earth, receiving less than 20 inches (50 cm) of rain a year, and they account for about one-fifth of the world's land. They are places of great extremes, going from incredibly hot to bitterly cold—often in the same day—which makes it a challenge for living things to survive there.

RED-TAILED HAWKS sometimes make their nests in cactuses Their diets include the snakes and lizards they find in the desert.

THE SONORAN DESERT

CACTUSES have thick skins and prickly spines that discourage animals from eating them.

The SIDEWINDER RATTLESNAKE slithers sideways by pressing only a small amount of its body against the sand—the better to avoid the hot ground!

But lots of fascinating plants and animals *do* survive, despite the sandy soil and harsh conditions. Most of the animals are meat-eaters, because there's so little plant life. The plants that are able to grow in the desert are especially good at storing water for a long time.

People live in deserts, too. They often travel from place to place to find water, or build man-made lakes called **reservoirs**, where they store the water they need for survival.

THE KALAHARI DESERT

CAMELS sweat only when it's very, very hot, so they can go for long periods without water. Their humps store fat, so they don't need to eat often, either.

The KALAHARI GROUND SQUIRREL has a large, bushy tail that it uses like a beach umbrella for shade.

GERBILS spend most of the daytime underground, coming out at night when it's cooler.

Going to Extremes

What to you think of when you hear the word *desert*? Vast distances of nothing but sand, in dunes stretching like waves to the horizon? Clear, blue, cloudless skies? No cities, no towns, no plants or trees (or very few)?

Well, that's a pretty good description of some deserts, but not all. Sand dunes—big, drifting mountains of sand—are found only rarely. More often, the desert surface is simply hard-packed soil. The one thing that all deserts have in common is that they are **arid**, which just means that they are both hot and dry. Some deserts are actually quite rainy, receiving perhaps 40 inches (100 centimeters) a year, but their high temperatures lead to high evaporation—which makes them arid.

Clouds are like blankets—they keep heat from escaping. But deserts have few clouds, so the daytime heat escapes easily at night. As a result, although deserts can get very hot in the day, they can get very cold at night, too—temperatures dropping by as much as 50 degrees Fahrenheit (28 degrees Celsius).

Another feature of deserts is that they are extremely windy. With very few plants and trees to get in the way, winds blow very hard. This can lead to sandstorms, when the wind carries away the loose soil and sand.

People can sometimes change the conditions in deserts. Did you know that some of the Earth's most productive farms are found in irrigated deserts? These are places where groundwater is brought to the surface or water is piped in from wetter areas. **Irrigation** can provide enough water to support large desert cities, including Las Vegas, Nevada. Much of the water used in Riyadh, the capital and largest city in Saudi Arabia, is piped in from the Persian Gulf after the salt is removed.

It's tough for life to survive in a desert, so the plants and animals that do survive—and even thrive—have developed special characteristics.

SAVE THE EARTH!

AS WE'VE LEARNED, YOU DON'T HAVE TO LIVE IN A DESERT TO CONSERVE WATER. TRY KEEPING A PITCHER OF WATER IN THE FRIDGE. THAT WAY, WHEN YOU'RE THIRSTY, YOU DON'T HAVE TO RUN THE FAUCET UNTIL THE WATER IS COOL ENOUGH TO DRINK—AND YOU'LL SAVE WATER THAT OTHERWISE WOULD HAVE JUST GONE DOWN THE DRAIN.

DISCOVER for YOURSELF
Make Tasty Sun Tea

Just as people, plants, and animals in the desert adapt to the hot and dry conditions, we can adapt–and even benefit–from the sun's warming rays. This easy recipe for Sun Tea uses the sun's heat to make a favorite summer drink.

You'll need:
- 1 gallon (4 liters) water
- 6 tea bags (ordinary tea, or try an herbal kind such as peppermint or a fruit flavor)
- A clear 1-gallon jug or pitcher

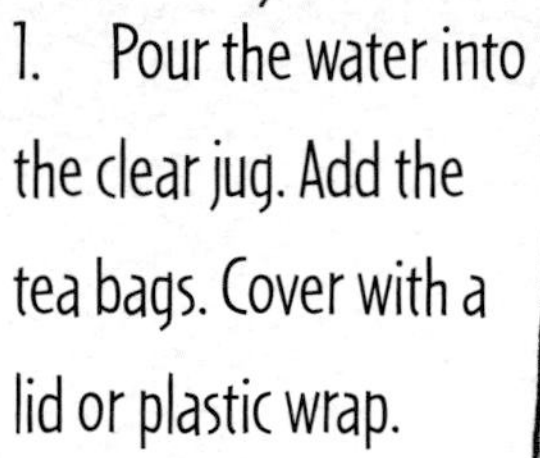

1. Pour the water into the clear jug. Add the tea bags. Cover with a lid or plastic wrap.
2. Leave the jug outside in the bright sun until the water is amber colored (usually just two or three hours). Remove the tea bags.
3. Refrigerate the jug and drink the tea within the next day or two. And that's it!

The sun does the work that a stove usually would, heating the water as it absorbs the tea's flavor! Add some ice, some sugar, and a bit of lemon or other fruit juice–*aaah*.

Survival of the Fittest

The seeds of some plants, such as CACTUSES, can live through long periods of no rain, then grow when rain finally falls. The root systems of desert plants are either very deep, so they can reach water far below the surface, or very wide, so they have access to more water when rain falls.

BATS and some FOXES and SNAKES come out at night when it's cooler.

Some mammals—such as MULE DEER and JACKRABBITS—have large ears that help them get rid of heat faster.

Desertification: Left High and Dry

1 Cattle eat all the plants in a field.

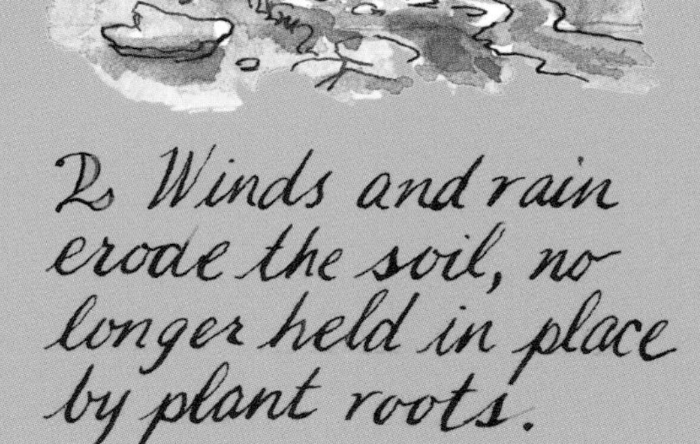

2 Winds and rain erode the soil, no longer held in place by plant roots.

3 The soil that is left is unable to support life.

In many places in the world, deserts are expanding. We call this **desertification**—the spread of desertlike conditions into neighboring areas.

This happens naturally sometimes, over thousands, even millions, of years. That type of desertification is mostly due to slow changes in the **climate**—the average weather conditions of a particular area.

But the desertification that people are worried about now is caused by us humans. Growing crops and allowing cows and sheep to graze can use up all of the natural plant life that wild animals once fed on. And that's not the only problem. Once the plants are gone, the ground erodes much faster.

What can we do about erosion? It's a tough problem that requires thinking big. Governments can encourage farmers to rotate their crops so the land can recover, for example, and food aid can be given to those who otherwise have no choice but to overuse the land. Like many problems facing the planet, erosion is one that we all need to work together to try to solve.

Life in the Freezer

THE ARCTIC

The coldest places on Earth are the South Pole (the continent of Antarctica) and the northern regions of Asia and North America. Surprisingly, these two places in the north are even colder than the North Pole, an area that is covered not by land but by water during the summer and floating ice in the winter.

Much of the ground in the Arctic is always frozen, and only special vegetation can grow here. Plants with short roots, such as COTTON GRASS, can survive in the thin, topmost layer of soil that thaws in summer.

The ARCTIC TERN is an amazing traveler. It spends summers in the Arctic, then flies south, all the way to the Antarctic, as the seasons change. As winter approaches in

POLAR BEARS have a thick layer of fat called blubber beneath their fur that helps protect them from the cold. Big animals conserve heat better than small ones do, and polar bears can grow to weigh 1,800 pounds (815 kilograms)!

The ARCTIC FOX spends its summers storing up food that it will need to last it through the long, cold winter.

SEALS swim in the cold Arctic Ocean. Their bodies store oxygen very well, so they can stay underwater for up to 30 minutes while searching for fish!

Because the very top and bottom of the planet are angled away from the sun for part of the year, these places get very little sunlight—or none at all—during their winters (which start in December in the north and June in the south). And at the height of their summers, it is bright all day but still quite cool.

The North and South poles are different in an important way. The South Pole—the southernmost point on the planet—is on Antarctica, which is a giant continent covered almost entirely by ice.

The North Pole, on the other hand, is in the Arctic Ocean. Despite the cold, some animals still are able to survive in both the Arctic and Antarctica.

the Antarctic, the tern makes the journey back north—a round-trip that can stretch to more than 22,000 miles (35,400 kilometers)!

THE ANTARCTIC

PENGUINS live in the Antarctic and huddle together for warmth. It's coldest on the outside of their circles, so they take turns standing in the middle.

BALEEN WHALES can be found in oceans throughout the world—including the cold waters near the Poles.

The Ice Ages

For reasons no one is completely certain of (scientists know a lot about the environment, but there still is a lot to learn!), the Earth has sometimes gotten very cold for a while. During these periods, lasting hundreds of thousands of years and called **ice ages**, ice covered great portions of the land, especially in the northern half of the planet.

During these ice ages, giant **continental ice sheets** spread from the poles toward the equator. Some of them were thousands of feet (hundreds of meters) thick, and they slowly carved out valleys as they slid south from the Arctic or north from the Antarctic. Dirt and boulders froze into the ice sheets as they moved along the planet's surface. In this way, great chunks of the Earth have been moved from one place to another, and the Earth's surface has been reshaped.

This movement was very slow—you wouldn't notice it moving if you were watching an ice sheet—but they did move, anywhere from a few yards or meters to a few hundred over the course of a year. When the ice age ended and the ice sheets disappeared, the valleys they carved remained, as did the dirt and boulders that they dragged with them.

HAVE AN ICE TIME

Here's something that may surprise you: Because there are continental ice sheets today, in places such as Greenland, some say we're in an ice age now. But most people use this term to describe times when ice sheets covered larger areas of the Earth.

Discover for Yourself
Make Your Own Ice Sheet

As the Earth's climate changes—both through natural processes and through man's impact on the environment—many ice sheets are retreating, and changing the landscape as they do. Are you curious about how ice sheets move and the things they leave behind? You can make a mini ice sheet at home and watch how it affects the surface as it moves.

You'll need:

- A clean plastic cup (an empty yogurt container works well)
- Sand, dirt, and pebbles
- Water
- A freezer
- A board at least 6 inches (15 cm) wide and 18 inches (45 cm) long
- A hammer and a nail
- A big, loose rubber band
- A brick

Start by filling your cup with an inch (2 cm) of sand, dirt, and pebbles. Then fill it with 2 inches (5 cm) of water. Put the cup in the freezer and remove it once the liquid has frozen. Then add another inch (2 cm) of sand, dirt, and pebbles and 2 more inches (5 cm) of water. Freeze it again. Continue this until you've filled the cup all the way up.

You've got your mini ice sheet; now you've got to prepare the surface it will move across. Have an adult hammer the nail into the top of your board. Then remove your mini ice sheet from the plastic cup. (Running a little hot water over the cup may help loosen it up.) Put your mini ice sheet on the board with the bigger side down.

Loop one end of the rubber band around the nail and the other end around the mini ice sheet. Then go outside and prop one end of the board—the end with the nail on it—on top of your brick. Now all you have to do is wait.

As your ice sheet melts, it will become lighter, and the rubber band will pull it slowly up the board. As this happens, it will leave behind the things that were frozen inside. Some of those things will slide down the board. Once the mini ice sheet has melted completely, all that will be left is a trail of dirt, sand, and pebbles—just like the deposits that are left when a real ice sheet melts.

The Air Around Us

Imagine that you've jumped into a swimming pool. When you're completely under, all at once everything feels very different. You feel the water pressing all over your body. And, depending on the temperature of the water, you feel colder or warmer. You also can't breathe!

You know that water is a fluid—but before you jumped into the pool, you were also in a fluid: the air around you! A fluid can be a liquid or a gas. In a pool, you feel the pressure of the water on your skin and its temperature. Standing outside the pool, you probably aren't aware of the pressure of the air, because you're used to it. But the air presses on your body just as water does. And you *do* often notice the temperature of the air—especially when you're hot in the summer or cold in the winter.

The air around us is a mixture of gases, mostly nitrogen and oxygen, called the **atmosphere**. We can measure its temperature and its **air pressure**, or how strongly it is pressing against us.

You know that you can't breathe when you are under water. That's because our bodies are built to breathe in the gases in the atmosphere around us—oxygen in particular. In the water, you are surrounded by a liquid. You can't breathe that because you're not a fish! And water is made mostly of hydrogen, but our bodies need to breathe in oxygen. The Earth's atmosphere is special because it has just the gases that we and the rest of the planet's forms of life need—and it's why we couldn't live on any other planet without somehow controlling the atmosphere around us.

Smog

You've probably heard the word *smog* before, and it's an easy one to define—combine "smoke" and "fog" and you get "smog." Smog is a form of pollution that makes the air seem hazy and dirty, and sometimes even smelly.

But where does smog come from? When fog mixes with smoke from, for example, a chimney, it can become a gray mist that floats over the ground. That's smog. But there are other ways to produce smog. Factories and automobiles often release **toxic**, or harmful, gases into the air. When sunlight hits these toxic gases, harmful clouds are produced that we call smog, too. Smog is most common in warm places with lots of cars and factories—such as large cities in Southern California or the southwest United States.

We've learned how special the air around us is, and how important it is for us to take care of it. Here's an easy and interesting way to see how smog—that dirty combination of smoke and fog—affects the air you breathe every day.

You'll need:
- 2 wire coat hangers
- 4 rubber bands
- A plastic bag

1. Bend the hangers so that they are shaped more like a square than a triangle.

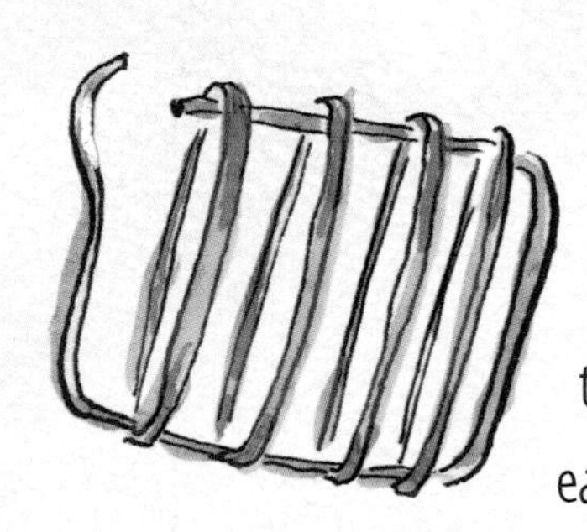

2. Put four rubber bands, evenly spaced, on each hanger. (You can make some minor adjustments to the shape of the hanger so that each rubber band is tight.)

DISCOVER for YOURSELF Make a Smog Detector

3. Hang one hanger outside in a spot where it will be shaded from the sun–a low-hanging tree branch, for example.

4. Put the other hanger inside the plastic bag and put it inside a drawer in your bedroom.

5. Wait for one week.

6. Take your "inside" hanger outdoors and compare it with the "outside" hanger. Stretch the rubber bands on each and see if you can tell any differences. (If you don't notice any differences yet, put the hangers back in their spots and wait another week.)

What you'll probably notice is that the rubber bands from the outside hanger have become cracked and brittle. If you pull on them, they may break. Why? Because smog has been eating away at them. The rubber bands on the inside hanger, meanwhile, are still in good shape because they've been protected indoors.

Smog seems a little more real when you see what it can do–right in your own backyard.

Remember the things you can do to help fight smog, such as bicycling or walking instead of riding in the car. You can also cut down on the power you use to reduce the amount of pollution power plants release into the air. We can fight smog if we all chip in.

As you might guess, smog isn't good for you. It can cause eye irritation and breathing problems such as asthma. Plants, trees, and other vegetation can also be harmed by smog.

WORKING TOGETHER

To reduce the amounts of pollutants we send into the atmosphere, we all have to make changes in how we live. Nations have to produce goods and generate power in new ways, and all of us have to change our habits, too, by doing things such as using less energy and driving less. It's not too late to slow down or even stop the damage being done to the environment—as long as countries agree to work together, and each of us does our part, too.

Grasping the Gravity of the Situation

As we've learned, all living things require environments that have just the right temperature and air pressure. These conditions have to be duplicated in the vehicles we send into space. Think about an astronaut's spacesuit—it's there to provide just the right temperature and air pressure. A space capsule or shuttle has to provide these conditions, too, almost like a giant spacesuit for a group of astronauts.

But the one thing that cannot easily be provided is gravity. So astronauts have had to learn to get along without it. Are you perhaps thinking that gravity has nothing to do with the atmosphere? Not so! It's gravity that holds the atmosphere to the Earth. Think about what would happen if gravity were to disappear—we, and the atmosphere around us, would all float off into space!

GRANDMA ENDURES A ZERO-GRAVITY MOMENT

How YOU can help!

Hitting the Brakes on Smog

Cars built today release fewer toxic gases than those built in the past. Some cars can run on **ethanol,** a fuel that can be made from corn and that burns more cleanly than gasoline. In the future, cars may run on hydrogen, which is plentiful and cheap. But today, most cars still run on gasoline, which causes them to release harmful gases as they burn fuel–gases that contribute to global warming. This is why many conservationists encourage us to use cars only when necessary. How can you help?

- **CARPOOL**. If your parents drive you to school, try starting a neighborhood carpool by sharing a ride with friends who live nearby. Ask your parents if they would volunteer to drive you and the other students from your neighborhood to school for a week. The next week, see if a friend's parent can do the driving. By taking turns, you're keeping more cars off the road–and producing less smog.

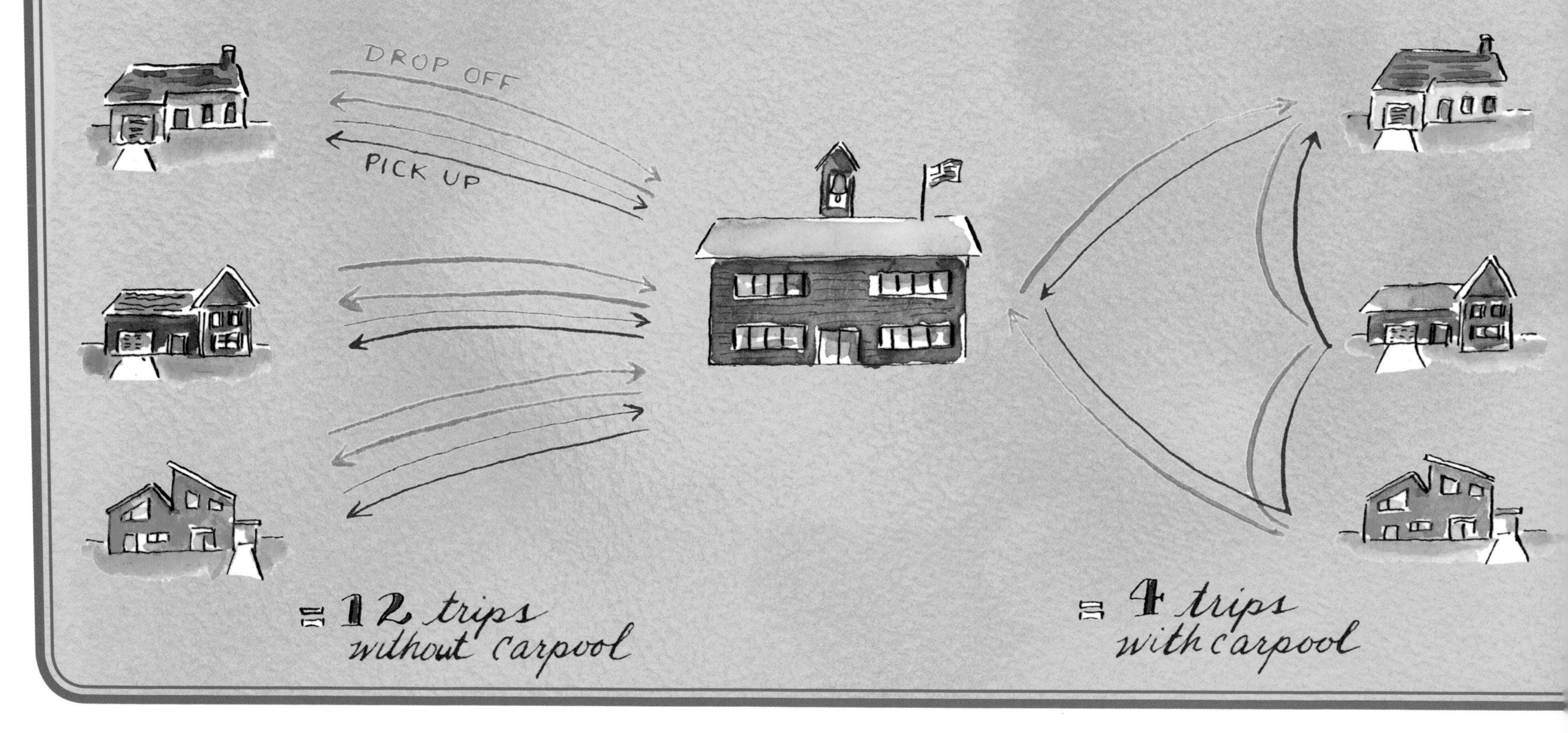

• **GO HYBRID**. Recently, cars that burn less gasoline have been growing in popularity. They are called **hybrids**, which describes something that is a combination of two or more things. Hybrid cars are part battery powered, part gas powered. This reduces the amount of gasoline they burn. You might or might not be able to persuade your parents to switch to cars that burn less gasoline–but it's something to remember someday when you buy a car.

• **WALK OR BIKE**. In the meantime, you can reduce your car use–and get good exercise–by walking or riding your bicycle rather than asking your parents for a ride in the car. The amount of toxic gas that car ride would release into the air might be small, but lots of small actions can lead to big changes. When it comes to protecting the planet–and your health–every little bit helps!

Weather Wisdom

Think of weather as what the atmosphere decides to do with itself. Should I make some rain today, or maybe a thunderstorm? Or should I take the clouds away and be sunny? Maybe I should get wild and make a hurricane, or a tornado!

The Earth's weather is the result of what's going on in the atmosphere. It all has to do with the transfer of energy. The sun is the source of this energy, but its rays hit different parts of the planet at different angles. This, among other factors, creates temperature differences from place to place, which the processes involved in weather attempt to equalize.

For example, the sun provides more heat to the low latitudes (near the equator) than the high latitudes. Then the heat naturally moves away from the equator toward the poles, causing great, swirling storms to sweep across the middle latitudes. These storms—the worst ones are called hurricanes—move cold air toward low latitudes and warm air toward high latitudes. This process is called "heat transfer."

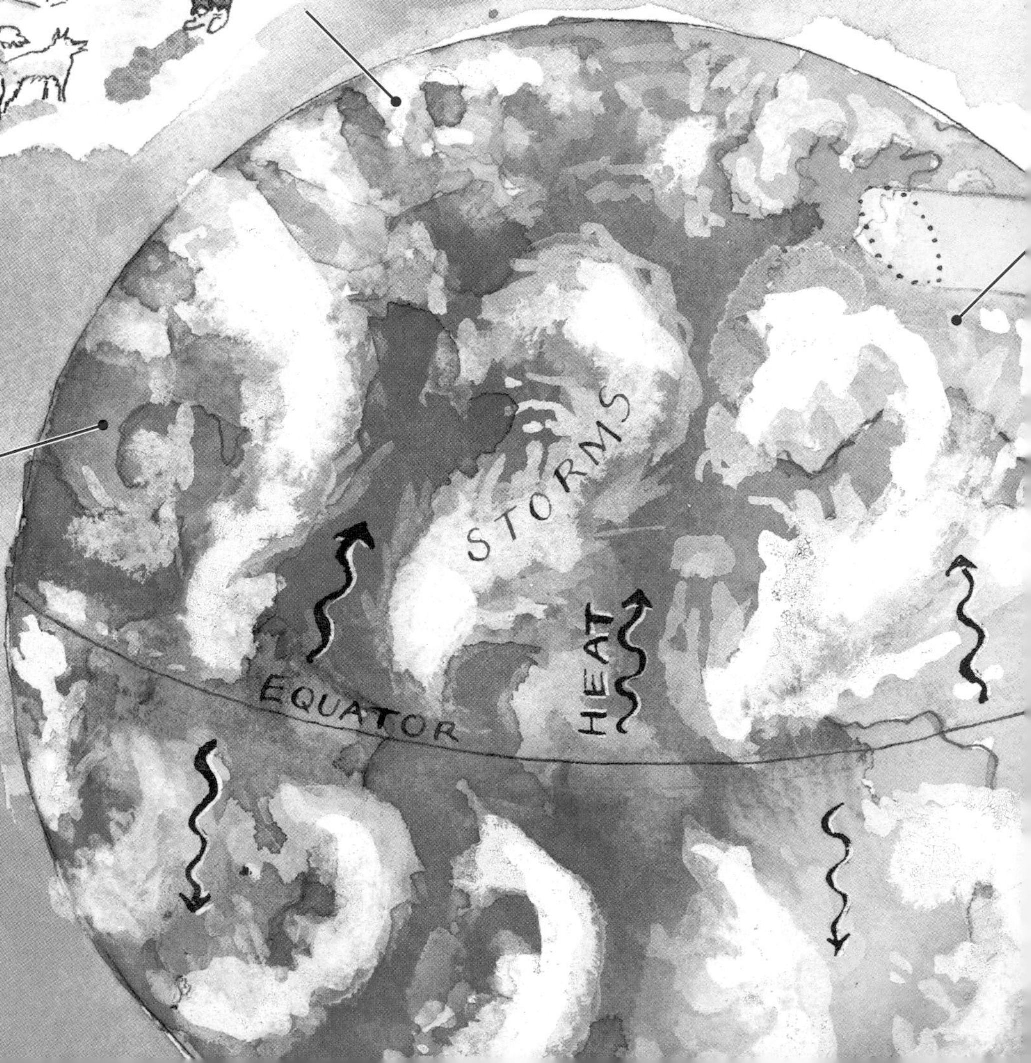

But what causes plain old thunderstorms? The Earth's surface is heated by the sun, which makes the lower atmosphere warmer than the higher atmosphere. This temperature difference—warm down and cold up—has to be equalized to get heat from downstairs to upstairs. So we have thunderstorms and other kinds of rain, the last step in a process that transfers heat from the lower atmosphere to the upper atmosphere. Sometimes this type of energy transfer becomes very powerful within a small area, and the result is a tornado.

There's no escape from the weather, and man has spent his entire lifetime—ever since he lived in caves—trying to avoid wet, windy, cold, hot, or stormy weather. We build houses, factories, teepees, and tents to protect ourselves from it, and use air conditioners and heaters to make the temperature more to our liking.

But we also use weather to our advantage when we can. We depend on rainfall to grow our crops, for example. We use water, wind, and sunlight to generate power. The fact is, there's hardly any weather that doesn't affect us in one way or another.

Cooler

Hotter and more direct

DISCOVE

Two Experiments to Help You

MAKE YOUR OWN LIGHTNING

Those flashes we see in the sky during thunderstorms–lightning–are really just giant sparks. The sparks are caused when electricity flows between clouds, or between a cloud and the ground. You can make your own spark (though much smaller and safer than lightning) at home with just a few tools.

You'll need:

- A sheet of newspaper
- A piece of plastic wrap
- A metal lid from a large coffee or other can (Be careful of the sharp edges!)
- A friend

1. Cover the palm of your hand with the plastic wrap.
2. Rub it back and forth quickly on the newspaper for about 30 seconds.
3. With your other hand, put the top of the metal can in the center of the newspaper.
4. Lift up the newspaper while your friend puts a finger near the metal.
5. Watch that spark! (It looks even more like lightning if you turn the lights out first!)

When you rubbed the newspaper, you charged it with **static electricity**. When your friend touched the lid, the electricity was released and it traveled from the newspaper to the lid. (Electricity flows easily through metal.) Lightning is just a much bigger version of this spark!

For YOURSELF
Understand How Weather Works

CHANGE THE AIR PRESSURE

Here's an "eggstreme" weather experiment. We know that the high winds in tornadoes can cause destruction –but the *low* air pressure they bring can be dangerous, too. Here's an easy way to experience the power of an air pressure drop.

You'll need:

- A peeled, hard-boiled egg
- A glass bottle with a neck slightly smaller than the egg (like an apple juice bottle)
- 3 or 4 matches
- A grownup to help

1. Have the grownup light the matches and drop them quickly into the bottle.
2. Place the egg on top of the bottle with the pointy side down, so that it completely fills the opening.
3. Watch what happens!

THUNK–the egg is pulled into the bottle! Why does this happen? First, the lit matches heat the air inside the bottle, using up the oxygen as they burn. When they go out, the air cools down, causing the air pressure inside the bottle to drop. But the air pressure outside remains the same–and the egg is sucked into the bottle!

In the case of a tornado, a drop in pressure can be harmful when it occurs on one side of a structure but not the other. This can cause the roof and walls to collapse inward, just like the egg was pulled inward.

Tornadoes, Hurricanes, and Other Extremes

The weather that makes news is usually the extreme kind: heat waves or cold blasts, drenching downpours, crippling blizzards, or dangerous tornados.

When we get hit with heavy **precipitation** (rain, snow, or hail), it is because of a number of things happening at more or less the same time. First, there has to be a lot of water vapor in the air that can condense—the more water vapor, the more precipitation. The next factor is the instability of the atmosphere. Remember that the atmosphere is always trying to equalize itself—to balance out high temperatures and low temperatures, high air pressure and low air pressure. For example, when a warm area with low air pressure meets a cold area with high air pressure, a lot of equalizing has to happen quickly in one place—and this can cause extreme weather. Each form of extreme weather has its own special causes and effects.

A **tornado** is a rotating cylinder of air with very high winds that circle around a small center of very low pressure. During especially strong thunderstorms, tornadoes form in a cloud when a pocket of warm air rises, swirling around and sucking in more air beneath it. That spinning air creates a funnel that descends to the ground. The funnel of a tornado can be anywhere from a few yards or meters to as much as 2 miles

(3 kilometers) wide. It can travel along the ground for less than 1 mile (1.5 kilometers), or for dozens. The very high-speed winds—up to 300 miles (almost 500 kilometers) per hour!—and severe drops in pressure as the tornado passes are what make a tornado so destructive. Tornados usually don't last very long, perhaps just a few minutes, although some have been observed to last for hours.

A **hurricane** is a circular area of low pressure much larger than a tornado that occurs when storm systems come together around a single area of very low pressure. A hurricane usually forms over the oceans of the lower latitudes in the late summer, when those waters are at their warmest. (The warmth of the water helps fuel the hurricane's power.) The winds and rains of a hurricane may extend for hundreds of miles or kilometers, though the most damaging forces are usually within a few dozen miles or kilometers around the eye of the storm. Hurricane winds can blow as fast as 125 miles (200 kilometers) per hour, and they bring incredible amounts of rain, which can cause a lot of damage. The big wall of water that a hurricane pushes in front of it is called a storm surge.

A **thunderstorm** includes heavy rainfall, high winds, thunder, and lightning. Thunderstorms sometimes bring **hail**, too, which is water that has frozen in the cold upper atmosphere before falling to the ground as ice. Hail can seem really strange, because it often falls when it's warm at ground level! It can range from the size of a pea to the size of a softball, and can cause damage wherever it lands.

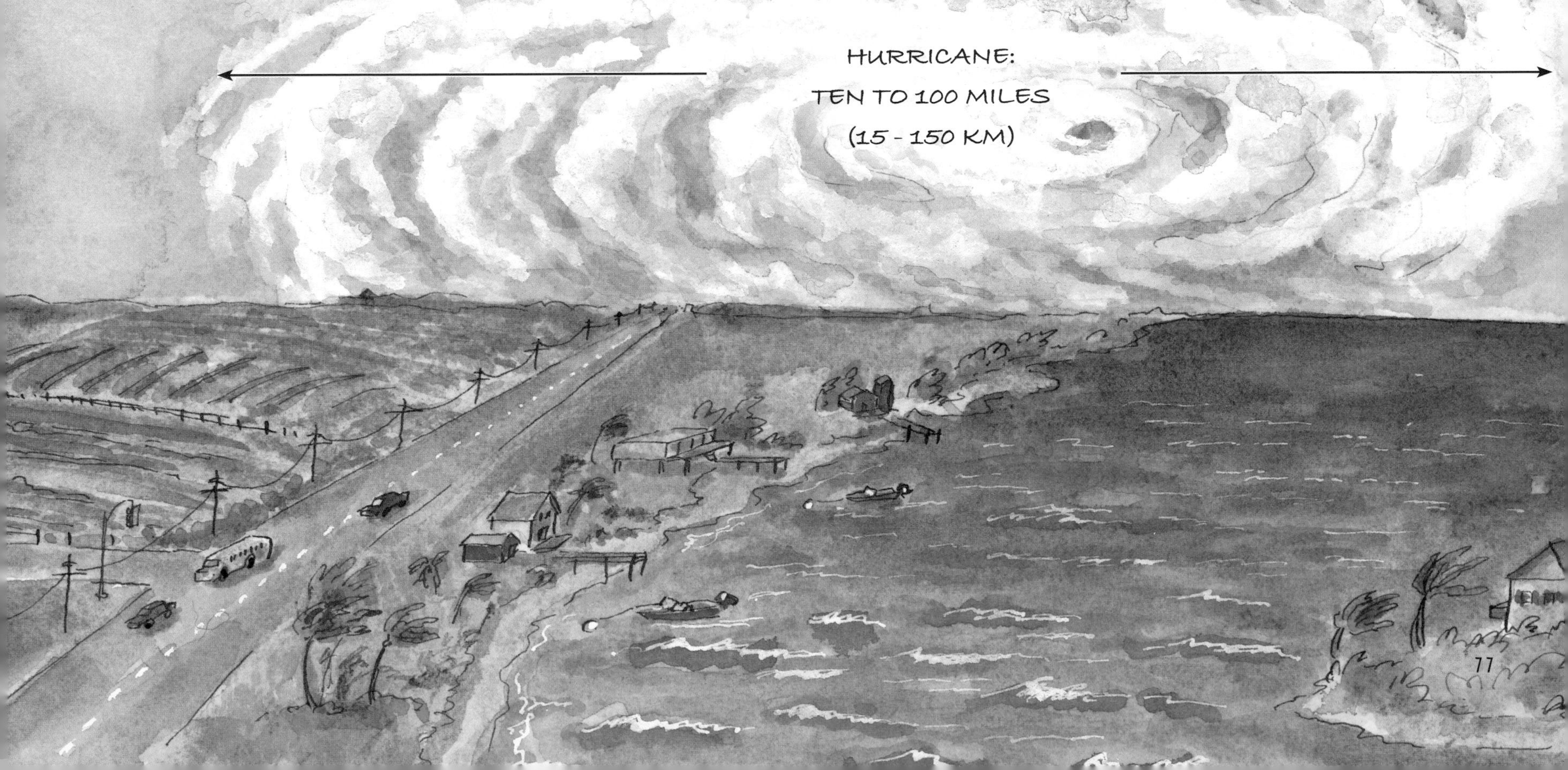

Global Warming and Acid Rain

Global Warming

You've probably heard the term **global warming,** which means just what it sounds like: The entire Earth system—including our atmosphere—is getting warmer.

The cause of this warming appears to be the increasing amount of certain gases—especially carbon dioxide—that are released into the atmosphere. This increase is due mainly to factories, power plants, and gasoline-burning vehicles that send gases into the atmosphere when fossil fuels are burned.

Carbon dioxide and the other gases that contribute to global warming are called **greenhouse gases** because they cause the atmosphere to act like a greenhouse, which is a house made of glass so the sun's energy can shine through and warm the inside. The glass lets the sun's rays in, but also helps keep some of the heat inside from escaping, so the air inside the greenhouse gets hotter than the air outside it. If you've ever gotten into a hot car on a sunny day, you've experienced the greenhouse effect. When a closed car stands out in the sun on a warm day, the air inside heats up but can't escape—so it's much hotter inside the car than outside.

Greenhouse gases act like the glass of that car, allowing the sun's rays to shine through but preventing some of the heat from escaping into space. As a result, the Earth warms up. We call this the **greenhouse effect**. Solid pollution in the atmosphere (such as dust, soot, and ash) also contributes to the greenhouse effect. The greenhouse effect isn't necessarily a bad thing—if the atmosphere didn't help contain some of the warmth we receive from the sun, we'd all freeze! But as we humans send more greenhouse gases and pollution into the atmosphere, our summers get hotter. As the oceans grow warmer, they start to melt the polar ice caps. This makes the sea levels rise and—unless we slow down or stop this process—eventually, the higher seas will bump into cities along the coasts. Global warming also causes weather changes. We are starting to have more **droughts** (dry spells) in some places and more rain in others.

Acid Rain

We've learned about some ways that human actions have contributed to environmental problems such as global warming. There are other problems that we all should know about, too, because a problem can't be solved until we understand it.

Acid rain is one of these problems. We know that gases are released into the atmosphere when fossil fuels are burned, and that they contribute to global warming. But these gases affect the rain, too. When the gases dissolve in clouds, they can change the chemical makeup of the water in those clouds, making it more acidic.

When that cloud later falls as rain, it can cause problems wherever it lands. Acid rain usually isn't harmful enough to injure people, but over time it can eat away at things that are exposed to it—a statue, for instance. More troubling is when acid rain falls into a lake or stream. Then it can change the water, making it difficult—or impossible—for certain plants and animals to survive. Burning less fossil fuels will help the acid rain problem, as well as help fight global warming.

Up, Up, and Away

Let's take a trip upward through the atmosphere and see how conditions change. This will have to be a pretend trip, because if we actually tried this without lots of protection, we'd be goners before we got up even a few miles or kilometers. It's awfully cold up there!

Let's start on a pleasant summer day, with temperatures around 70 degrees Fahrenheit (20 degrees Celsius). The first change we notice as we climb is that the temperature drops—we can feel it getting cooler. This is because the immediate source of heat for the Earth is its surface, which absorbs the sun's rays and heats up. So the closer we are to the surface, the warmer it is. Before too long, maybe at 8,000 to 10,000 feet (2,400–3,000 meters), we begin to climb through clouds. We can see that these are the puffy type called cumulus (pronounced *KYEWM-you-lus*) clouds. Not only can we see them up close, but we get wet! As we've learned, we're bumping into millions of tiny water droplets.

Once we're through the cumulus clouds, still climbing, we begin to feel a little out of breath. Our hearts are beating faster, too. This is because there's less oxygen in the air than when we started our trip. Just as we need food for energy, we need oxygen to live. If this weren't an imaginary trip, we'd need an extra oxygen supply once we got to a height of about 12,000 to 15,000 feet, or about 3,650 to 4,570 meters.

Now we're up to about 30,000 feet (9,100 meters)—or almost 6 miles (10 kilometers) up—and it's getting colder all the time. Suddenly we bump into the bottom of another layer of clouds. Because it's so cold at this level, the water vapor is frozen, and what we've bumped into are cirrus (pronounced *SERE-us*) clouds. Instead of tiny water droplets, we're bumping into tiny pieces of ice.

Then we're through the cirrus clouds and still climbing. The air at this level has very little oxygen and it's very, very cold—the temperature is almost minus 100 degrees Fahrenheit (minus 73 Celsius)! The air pressure is also much less than back on Earth, and this would be harmful to our insides. Another thing that has changed drastically since we started our trip (whether we noticed it or not) is the amount of sunlight. The rays are very strong this high up, and we'd get a sunburn awfully fast—in fact, in about a minute! Our journey ends at about 48,000 feet (15,000 meters), where there's very little left of the atmosphere—almost no oxygen, carbon dioxide, or water vapor at all. Good thing this trip was just pretend!

Blowin' in the Wind

Man has been using the power of the wind for centuries. Sailing ships have traveled the world with nothing pushing them along but the ocean breeze. For hundreds of years, windmills have been used to grind crops such as corn. In more recent times, the wind has been used to generate electricity using **wind turbines.**

A wind turbine looks like a giant windmill. Just as the hydroelectric sources we learned about generate energy using flowing water, wind turbines use the wind.

WIND POWER, 1492

WIND POWER, 1800

WIND POWER, 1900

Wind turbines are pretty impressive to look at. They can be as tall as 350 feet (107 meters), with two or three blades measuring up to 165 feet (50 meters) long each. As the wind blows, the blades turn and the machinery inside the generator below produces energy. Wind turbines can be rotated to face the wind, and the blades can be adjusted to turn at the fastest rate possible.

ALTOGETHER, WIND FARMS IN THE UNITED STATES PRODUCE ENOUGH ENERGY TO POWER MORE THAN A MILLION AND A HALF HOUSEHOLDS!

Because wind turbines produce much less energy than the typical power plant that burns fossil fuels, they are clustered together in **wind farms**, collections of many wind turbines—sometimes thousands of them. Working together, they can produce much more energy than one wind turbine could alone.

The great thing about wind farms is that they rely entirely on a renewable resource—we'll never run out of wind. And they produce no pollution at all.

But they have some drawbacks: Some people have complained that wind turbines are noisy and not very pretty to look at. The bigger problem is that they only work well in very windy places, and it takes a large number of them to produce enough energy to be useful.

WIND POWER, PRESENT

Discover for Yourself
Build Your Own Wind Turbine

Want to see how a wind turbine can generate power? It's a lot easier than you think.

You'll need:
- A propeller with fixed blades. You'll find one on the end of pinwheels, or you could use the propeller from a toy helicopter. You may even be able to find propellers sold separately at hobby stores.
- A round rod about 2 feet (60 cm) long, thin enough to fit inside a drinking straw
- 1 nail
- A drinking straw
- A piece of string 3 feet (1 m) long
- A small, lightweight toy–an action figure, for example

1. Have your parents connect the propeller to the end of the rod using the nail. Make sure it's tight, so that the propeller can't spin without turning the rod.

2. Run the end of the rod through the straw.

3. Tie the string to the end of the rod behind the straw.

4. Tie the other end of the string to your toy.

5. Now you're ready to put your wind turbine the rod inside the straw. That will cause the string

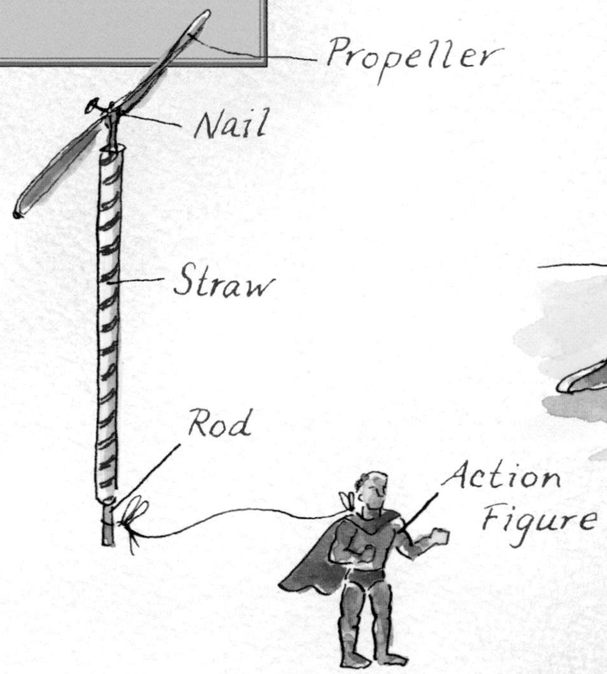

to slowly spool around the rod, and your toy will slowly rise up toward you. (You may need to experiment with different toys before you find one that is light enough for the turbine to lift.) Though it doesn't take much energy to lift a small toy, it can't rise on its own–so you've got the wind doing it for you. You've made a wind turbine that follows the same basic rules that giant turbines follow, using a renewable resource–the wind–and causing no pollution.

The Ozone Layer

Another problem that we humans have helped to cause is the shrinking of the ozone layer, the layer of oxygen about 15 miles (24 kilometers) above the Earth. The ozone layer helps protect us from the sun's rays—sort of like a layer of natural sunblock high above the ground!

Starting about thirty years ago, a hole in this layer has appeared above Antarctica every October. Hardly any people live there, so it hasn't caused a lot of harm to humans. But if the hole grows bigger, it might spread over places where more people live, exposing them to more of the sun's powerful rays. This could lead to worse sunburns, for one thing, but also to more serious problems such as skin cancer.

The good news is that the nations of the world are working to fix this problem. It's thought that the ozone hole was caused by chemicals used in Styrofoam, aerosol spray cans, refrigerators, and fire extinguishers. When those chemicals were released into the atmosphere, they broke down some of the ozone in the ozone layer. Most manufacturers are now making those products differently, so fewer harmful chemicals are released into the atmosphere.

Energy from the Sun, and Other Bright Ideas

We've learned how important the production of energy is. We've also learned that generating energy can sometimes have harmful effects on the planet. As we look to the future, scientists and others are searching for energy sources that don't harm the planet. Hydroelectric plants and wind farms are two such sources, but there are others, too.

The sun produces lots of energy—without its heat, none of us could survive. **Solar cells**, big panels that collect the power of the sun, change sunlight into electricity. They're put in very sunny places—on the roof of a house, for example—and are good sources of power for things such as heating the water in a house. They are also used on satellites in outer space. Solar power has its limits, though—solar cells only generate small amounts of electricity, and that electricity is difficult to store for later use.

Nuclear plants use special scientific methods to generate energy through complicated chemical reactions. The process they use releases a lot of energy from just a small amount of fuel. About 2 pounds (1 kilogram) of fuel in a nuclear plant can provide the same amount of energy as 2,000 tons (1,800 metric tons) of coal! And nuclear energy does not cause the pollution that fossil fuels do—though it can be dangerous if it is not handled carefully. Disposing of the **toxic** (poisonous) waste afterward is hard to do safely, too, but many people feel that our future depends on figuring out good, safe ways to use nuclear energy.

The rocks below the surface of the Earth are often hot, and **geothermal power plants** use this heat to generate power. The energy created through this method can be used to heat buildings and to create steam that turns generators. This can only be done in places where the hot rocks are fairly close to the Earth's surface—not much more than 2 miles (3 kilometers) down. Iceland is an example of a country that gets some of its energy from geothermal power plants.

We've Got the Whole World...

Well, we've reached the end of our journey around the planet. We've seen the frozen South Pole, the steamy tropical rain forests, the spooky depths of the ocean, and the lofty heights above the Earth's surface, where the oxygen disappears—and we've seen lots of stuff in between.

We've learned how animals and plants interact and how the atmosphere affects us all. We've learned about the different kinds of power and how much man has come to rely on them for survival. And, most important of all, we've seen how the planet is changing and what that might mean in the future. The more we know about our big, beautiful Earth, the better prepared we are to protect it for ourselves and for those who come after us. Whether it's planting a tree, fixing a leaky faucet, organizing a carpool, or just turning off an unwatched television, there are lots of things each one of us can do to help nurture and protect our home.

So, let's use all that we have discovered! Spread the word about the wonders of the world and what we can do to protect it. Remember, lots of *small* actions can lead to *big* changes! If we all work together, we can make sure the Earth stays the very special place it is.

15 Easy Things Everyone Can Do to Conserve Energy—and Help Save the Planet!

1. Turn off the lights when you leave a room.

2. Make sure your parents have the dishwasher set to energy-saving mode. Or, better yet, wash the dishes by hand if there are just a few of them, and let them air dry.

3. Turn off the computer when you're not using it. A computer doesn't use a lot of energy, but it adds up over time.

4. Never leave the television on when no one is watching it. Same goes for the radio.

5. Skip the hair dryer! Try letting your locks dry naturally.

6. Next time you're helping your parents cook, put a lid on that pot when you're boiling water. It will heat up much faster and use less energy.

7. Fill the fridge! Once the items inside get cold, they help *keep* the refrigerator cold, so it needs less power to maintain that temperature. (But don't *absolutely stuff* it, which will prevent the air inside from circulating properly.)

8. Try to get your family in the habit of using the washer and dryer only when they are full–not just for a couple of shirts and a pair of pants. This will save water *and* energy.

9. Don't heat or air-condition rooms that aren't being used–close the doors and ask your parents to close the heating/cooling vents in those rooms. When it's not *too* hot, try using a fan instead. When its not too cold, wear a sweater and leave the heat off.

10. Drive greener! Ask your parents to use the cruise control on the highway to keep a steady speed–frequently slowing down and speeding up burns more gas. Driving more slowly in the city will save gas, too.

11. Help your parents keep the correct amount of air in your car tires. Cars running at the right air pressure use less gas.

12. Don't carry extra junk inside the car or in the trunk. That burns more gas, too.

13. Here's a surprising way to save gas when it's hot out: Drive with the windows up and the air conditioner on! Studies have shown that the wind whipping through open windows slows a car down, burning more gas than it takes to run the air conditioner.

14. At school or in other buildings, take the stairs, not the elevator. This saves energy–and keeps your body in better shape, too!

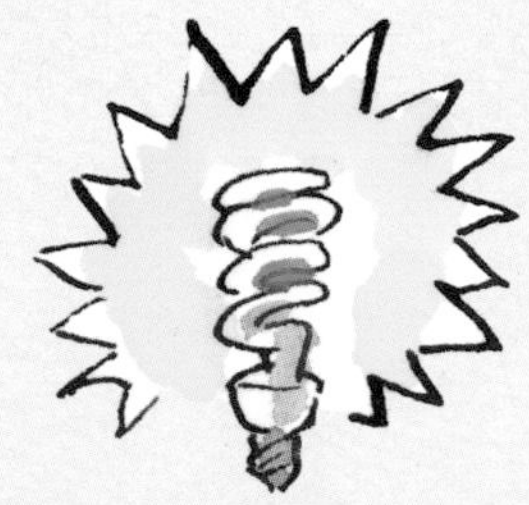

15. Use energy-saving fluorescent light bulbs. They cost a little more than other bulbs, but use about 75 percent less energy and last around ten times longer–meaning, in the long run, you save money *and* power!

Words for the Wise

Here's a handy glossary of all of the new words you learned in this book.

Air pressure – How strongly the atmosphere presses against something.

Amphibians – Animals that generally begin life in the water, breathing through gills, then move onto dry land and breathe through lungs.

Arid – Describes a place with low precipitation and high evaporation.

Aquifer – A place underground where water has collected.

Atmosphere – The mixture of gases, mostly nitrogen and oxygen, that makes up the air.

Birds – Warm-blooded animals that lay eggs, have a beak, and are covered with feathers.

Carnivores – Animals that eat other animals.

Climate – The average weather conditions in a particular area.

Compost – Decayed organic material that can be added to soil, making it healthier and more able to support new life.

Condensation – When water turns from gas to liquid.

Coniferous forest – A forest whose trees have needles that they keep year-round.

Conservationist – One who works to protect plants, animals, and the Earth's other natural resources.

Continental ice sheets – Large masses of ice that spread from the poles to the equator during an ice age.

Crops – Plants or animals raised by a farmer or rancher.

Currents – The movement of great streams of surface water from one place to another within the Earth's oceans, sometimes bringing warmer water to a cold place or vice versa.

Deciduous forest – A forest whose trees shed their leaves every year.

Desertification – The spread of desert-like conditions to areas that weren't deserts before.

Drought – A long period of dry weather.

Ecosystem – A collection of living things and the environment in which they live.

Electricity – A form of energy produced by tiny charged particles.

Erosion – The gradual wearing away of the ground, making an area unable to support new life.

Ethanol – A fuel made from corn, or other organic sources, that is used to power some cars.

Evaporation – When water turns from liquid to gas.

Evergreens – Trees found in coniferous forests.

Extinct –Refers to a plant or animal species that has disappeared from the Earth.

Fertile – Land that is in the right condition to support crops.

Fish – Cold-blooded animals that live in the water and use gills to get the oxygen they need.

Freshwater – Water with almost no salt in it, such as the water in most lakes, rivers, streams, and ponds.

Generator – A machine that uses moving parts to create electricity.

Geothermal power plant – A plant that uses the heat of rocks below the Earth's surface to generate power.

Global warming –Warming of the Earth caused, at least in part, by man's actions.

Greenhouse effect – When heat from the sun is trapped in the Earth's atmosphere.

Greenhouse gases –Gases in the atmosphere that contribute to the greenhouse effect.

Groundwater – Water found below the surface of the Earth.

Habitat – The area where a plant or animal species normally lives.

Hail – Ice that falls from the clouds, usually during a thunderstorm, even when the temperature is warm at ground level.

Herbivores – Animals that eat plants.

Hibernation – When animals sleep during winter months. This helps protect them from the cold and conserve energy during times when food is hard to find.

Hurricane – A circular area of low pressure that occurs when storm systems come together around an area of very low pressure.

Hybrids – Two things combined. Hybrid cars run on a combination of gasoline and battery power.

Ice age – A long period of time when ice covers a great portion of the land.

Irrigation –Bringing water to a dry area to grow crops or support daily life.

Landfill – A place where trash is dumped and covered with layers of dirt.

Latitude –A unit used for measuring distance north or south of the Earth's equator. Low latitudes are near the equator; high latitudes are farther from it.

Mammals – Warm-blooded animals that feed their young with milk they produce.

Mass transit – Transportation methods designed to move lots of people quickly and cheaply.

Mollusk – A soft animal with no spine, such as a clam or a snail, that often lives inside a hard shell.

Nuclear plant – A power plant that uses special scientific methods to generate electricity by splitting atoms.

Omnivores – Animals that eat both plants and animals.

Plankton – Very small (sometimes too small to see with your eyes) plants and animals that float in the water.

Photosynthesis – The process by which a plant makes sugar using water, carbon dioxide, and sunlight. It uses this sugar as food and releases oxygen into the atmosphere.

Pollution – Waste that dirties the land, air, or water.

Precipitation – Water such as snow, rain, or hail that falls during a storm.

Predator – An animal that eats another animal (its *prey*) for food.

Rain forest – A thick forest found close to the equator that receives a great deal of rain. Plants here grow all year long, and more than half of the animal and plant species in the world are found here.

Renewable – A resource that cannot be used up or can be naturally replaced, such as sunlight or water.

Reptiles – Cold-blooded animals, covered with scales or hard plates, that breathe through lungs.

Reservoir – A manmade lake used for storing water.

Rural – Communities that have lots of land but few people.

Salinity – A measure of the amount of salt dissolved in water.

Sea level – The point where the ocean meets the shore—and a standard for measuring the height of a mountain or the depth of an ocean.

Solar cell – A device that turns energy from the sun into electricity.

Species – A group of plants or animals that share certain characteristics.

Static electricity – An electrical charge that builds up in an object rather than flowing through it.

Storm surge – A sometimes destructive wall of seawater that is pushed forward in the direction in which a hurricane is moving.

Suburbs – Short for *suburban*, these are smaller communities built near cities.

Surface water – Water on the surface of the Earth, as in rivers or lakes.

Thunderstorm – a storm that includes heavy rainfall, high winds, and lightning.

Tornado – A rotating cylinder of air with very high winds circling around a small center of low pressure.

Toxic – Something that is harmful to people, plants, animals, or the Earth.

Wind farm – A collection of many wind turbines working together to provide energy.

Wind turbine – A large windmill-like machine used to generate electricity.

Read More About It

More About the Earth

Bishop, Keith. *Environment*. BBC Educational Publishing, 1996.

Catalano, Angela. *Community Space*. New York: The Rosen Publishing Group, Inc., 2005.

Johnston, Andrew K. *Earth From Space*. Ontario: Firefly Books, Ltd., 2007.

Kingfisher Science Encyclopedia. Boston: Kingfisher Publications PLC., 2006.

Marshak, Stephen. *Earth: Portrait of a Planet*. New York: W.W. Norton & Company, 2005.

Tarbuck, Edward J., and Frederick K. Lutgens. *Earth: An Introduction to Physical Geology*. New York: Pearson Education, Inc., 2005.

More About Experiments and Activities

Churchill, E. Richard, Louis V. Loeschnig and Muriel Mandell. *365 Simple Science Experiments*. New York: Black Dog & Leventhal Publishers, Inc., 1997.

EarthWorks Group. *50 Simple Things Kids Can Do to Save the Earth*. New York: Scholastic, Inc., 1990.

EarthWorks Group. *50 Simple Things You Can Do to Save the Earth*. Berkeley, California: Earthworks Press, 1989.

MacEachern, Diane. *Save Our Planet*. New York: Dell Publishing, 1990.

Schwartz, Linda. *Earth Book for Kids*. The Learning Works, Inc., 1990.

More About Animals

First Nature Encyclopedia. New York: DK Publishing, Inc., 2006.

Grzimek's Animal Life Encyclopedia. The Gale Group, Inc, 2005.

Kingfisher First Animal Encyclopedia. Boston: Kingfisher Publications Plc., 1998.

Read About It on the Web

AmericanForests.org

American Wind Energy Association (www.awea.org)

BluePlanetBiomes.org

ConsumerEnergyCenter.org

eNature.com

TheEnvironmentSite.org

Forestry.about.com

Geology.com

The Green Squad (www.nrdc.org/greensquad)

LivingRainforest.com

NASA'S For Kids Only (kids.earth.nasa.gov)

National Resources Defense Council (nrdc.org)

Rainforest Action Network (ran.org)

ZOOM (pbskids.org/zoom)

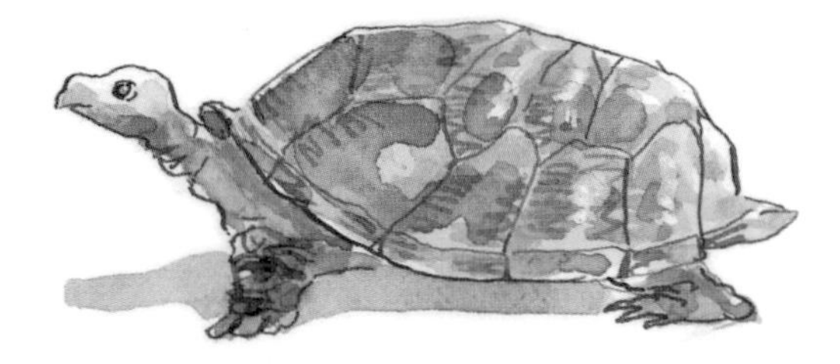

MICHAEL DRISCOLL is the author of *A Child's Introduction to Poetry* and *A Child's Introduction to the Night Sky*. He has contributed to Reuters, *The Village Voice* and *L.A. Weekly*, among other publications, and has received awards for his books and his newspaper writing. He has worked as an editor at Penguin USA and Black Dog & Leventhal, and is currently an editor at the *New York Daily News*. He lives in New York City. His father, DENNIS DRISCOLL, is an emeritus professor of meteorology at Texas A&M University, specializing in biometeorology, the interaction of the Earth's atmosphere with living things. He is the author of numerous scientific journal articles on how atmospheric conditions affect health and well-being. He lives in College Station, Texas.